MANAGEMENT OF FINANCIAL MARKET AFTER GLOBALISATION

MANAGEMENT OF FINANCIAL MARKET AFTER GLOBALISATION

By

Dr. R.N. Misra

Professor
Deptt. of Management
SMIT, Berhampur
Under Biju Patnaik University of Technology
Rourkela
(Orissa)

DISCOVERY PUBLISHING HOUSE PVT. LTD.
NEW DELHI-110 002

First Published-2010

ISBN 978-81-8356-591-2

© Author

Published by:

DISCOVERY PUBLISHING HOUSE PVT. LTD.
4831/24, Ansari Road, Prahlad Street
Darya Ganj, New Delhi-110002 (India)
Phone: 23279245, 43764432 • Fax: 91-11-23253475
E-mail: parul.wasan@gmail.com
info@discoverypublishinggroup.com
Website: www.discoverypublishinggroup.com

Printed at:

Arora Offset Press, Delhi – 92

Preface

Due to large size of population 60 million households are living below the poverty line in the country. These households depend mostly on credit. Unless the financial institutions provide credit to these needy persons to do their business/services activities, that will be no upliftment of their living standard. Rural poor are exploited by the rich persons of rural areas. After globalization the demand for credit have increases. Now more and more financial institutions came forward to provide credit needs to the needy persons by approaching their door steps. More than 50% persons borrows utilizes their funds taken from the institutional agencies in proper manner which help them to up life their standard of living and repayment of credit in time.

Other borrowers misutilize the fund in different manner, so they do not generate any income from the loan so they are not able to repay their credit in time, which not any create problems to the borrowers, but also to the banking institutions and Government at large which need due consideration.

Prof. R.N. MISRA

Acknowledgements

I am very much thankful to all paper contributors of this book.

I express my special thanks to Mr. Tilak Wasan, the owner of M/s. Discovery Publishing House, who has extended his help and co-operation and inspired me to write book. I really thankful to him.

I am also thankful to my wife Smt. Swarna Prava Misra and my sons Roopesh and Rookesh for their inspiration to write books. I am also very much thankful to my daughter-in-law Smt. Amrita Rani Misra in editing this book.

Last but not least, I am also thankful to Mr. Biswanath Patro, Faculty member of Computer Science, PGCMS, SMIT, Berhampur for his kind help and co-operation for editing this book.

Prof. R.N. MISRA

Contents

Preface *v*

Acknowledgements *vii*

1. **Financing the Self-help Groups by the Financial Institutions** **1**
   —*Anita Patra and Dr. R.N. Misra*

2. **Role of Cooperative Banks in Financing Agricultural Credit in Orissa** **13**
   —Dr. Sudhansu Sekhar Nayak and Dr. Rabi Narayan Misra

3. **Role of Financial Institutions in Economic Development of Orissa** **27**
   —*Prof. R.P. Sarma*

4. **Micro Finance in India** **38**
   —Prof. Rabi Narayana Mishra and Dr. Satyabrat Dash

5. **Regularities in Indian Stock Market: An Investigation** **57**
   —Harish Kumar and Dr. Malabika Deo

6. **Institutional Credit and Agricultural Development in Orissa** **79**
   —Bibhudatta Nayak

7. **Financial Derivative After Globalisation** **101**
   —*Sudhir Pradhan and Biswanath Patro*

8. **Changing Pattern of Panchayat Finance in Orissa: A Study** **120**
—Dr. Bhagabata Patro, Dr. Kishore Chandra Pattnaik and Bibhu Prasad Sahu

9. **Management of Financial Services in Orissa – A Look** **134**
—Dr. Anil Kumar Sahu

10. **Bank Finance Under Swarnajayanti Gram Swarojgar Yojana (SGSY)** **141**
—Mr. S.K. Badtiya and Dr. R.N. Misra

Index **151**

Financing the Self-help Groups by the Financial Institutions

—Anita Patra*

—Dr. R.N. Misra**

INTRODUCTION

Entrepreneurship contributes in the economic growth of a nation. Due to new small businesses there is an increase in productivity, there is promotion of innovative technologies, there is a change in the market place competition. Entrepreneurs are born out of the people who have high need for achievement, tolerance towards risk, tolerance towards ambiguity. Entrepreneurs are also created due to some sociological factors viz. discrimination against them in the society, either directly or indirectly.

In India, the patriarchal society has always oppressed the women. For long the status of women

* Sr. Lecturer, Centurion School of Rural Enterprise Management, Parlakhemundi, Gajapati District, Odisha.

** Professor, Sanjay Memorial Institute of Technology, Berhampur, Ganjam District, Odisha.

was different from that of men in terms of their roles and responsibilities both in family and the society. This led the Government to go for the women focused development programmes. Rural women's development received priority for the first time during the Sixth Plan period. A chapter on women and development was included for the first time in the Sixth Plan document. Targeting rural poor women in particular, the plan declared that, "a fair share of employment opportunities would have to be created through poverty alleviation programmes". The assumption continued to be that employment and income generation would automatically lead to improvement in the status of women. The two plans that followed noted that the result in this regard was not achieved commensurate to the inputs made. A separate ministry for women and children was created in 1984.

Under IRDP (Integrated Rural Development Programme) a special sub-programme called Development of Women and Children in Rural Areas (DWCRA) was started in 1982 to initiate women into group activities, encourage thrift and given them greater confidence to venture self-employment activities. Under the DWCRA Self-help Groups are formed. Self-help Groups (SHGs) are usually informal groups whose members have a common perception of need and importance towards collective action. National Bank for Agriculture and Rural Development (NABARD) defines SHGs as a group of 10 to 20 people from a homogeneous class who are willing to come together for addressing their common problems. These groups promote regular savings among members and use the pooled resources to meet the emergent needs of their members, including the consumption needs.

The groups meet regularly at one of the members place - it may be once in a month or fortnight or week. The process helps them to imbibe the essentials of financial intermediation including prioritization of needs, setting self-determined terms for repayment, keeping books and records. It builds financial discipline and credit history that then encourages banks to lend to them in certain multiples of their own savings and without any demand for collateral security.

NABARD launched a pilot project to provide micro credit by linking SHGs with banks in 1991-92. During the project period many NGOs came forward and have done excellent work in the promotion of SHGs and mobilization of thrift and disbursal of credit. In 1999, RBI had set up a Micro-credit cell to make it easier to provide Micro-credit providers to pursue institutional development process. Therefore, Micro-credit system has been considered as an important instrument to provide credit for self-employment and other financial and business services, including savings and technical assistance, to very poor people. The basic objectives address for the needy and poor people who seek small but urgent loans for consumption, production etc.

OBJECTIVE OF THE STUDY

The Self-help groups provide economic benefits in certain areas of production process by undertaking common action programmes, like cost-effective credit delivery system, generating a forum for collective, learning with rural people, promoting democratic culture, fostering an entrepreneurial culture, providing a firm base for dialogue and co-operation in programmes with other institutions, possessing credibility and power to ensure participation and helping to assess an individual member-s' management capacity. For the purpose of the study we have taken Gajapati District of Odisha as our study.

The objective of the study is to:

1. study the operational mechanism of the self-help Groups.
2. study the entrepreneurial growth through the self-help groups of the sample district.

Limitations of the Study

For the purpose of the study 800 samples were taken. The information provided by the beneficiaries are not 100% correct. Only one district was taken as sample district due to limitations of time and resources. The secondary data used for the purpose of the study has its own limitations.

BRIEF PROFILE OF THE SAMPLE DISTRICT

The district came into being with effect from 2nd October, 1992 by the Government of Odisha Notification No. 48522, dated 28th September, 1992. Prior to this date it was a part of Ganjam district. The district has a geographical area of 4,443.99 sq. km, the total forest area is 2,351.11 sq. km. The population (as per 2001 Census) was 5,18,448, of which male is 2,55,288 and female is 2,63,160. The urban population is 52,773 of which the males are 26,528 and females are 26,245. The rural population is 4,65,675, of which males are 2,28,760 and females are 2,36,915. Out of the total population 2,61,906 (around 50%) are

Schedules Tribes (ST) and 30,358 (around 6%) are Scheduled Castes (SC). The number of B.P.L. families is 68,763. The district consists of one Sub-Division, three tehasils, seven blocks, one NAC and one municipalities, 129 Gram Panchayats, 1583 villages. Out of the total population 4,65,949 are from the seven blocks.

THE METHODOLOGY

The study is exploratory study. For the purpose of the study primary data was collected by interviewing the beneficiaries (the members of the SHGs) using questionnaires. To make the study more effective focus group discussions were also made with the SHGs. The data was collected from SHGs of all the seven blocks of the district Gajapati. Total sample size is 800. The data collected are tabulated.

ANALYSIS OF THE STUDY

The growth of SHGs in the country is explained in Table 1.1.

Table 1.1: Growth of SHGs in India from 1992-1999 to 2005-2006 (Cumulative progress)

Year	SHGs number	Growth of SHGs	Bank loans (amount in million)	Growth in the amount of loans (amount in million)
1992-99	32,995	32,995	570	570
2000-01	1,49,050	2,63,825	2,880	4,810
2002-03	2,55,882	7,17,360	10,230	20,490
2003-04	3,61,731	10,79,091	18,552	39,042
2004-05	5,39,365	1,618,456	29,943	68,985
2005-06	6,20,109	2,238,565	44,990	1,13,975

Source: Southern Economist, November 1, 2008.

Table 1.2: Region wise growth of SHGs linked to the banks of the country (Cumulative growth)

Region	March 2001	March 2002	March 2003	March 2004	March 2005	March 2006
Northern Region	9,012	19,321	34,923	52,396	86,018	133,097
North-Eastern Region	477	1,490	4,069	12,278	34,238	62,517
Eastern Region	22,252	45,892	90,893	158,237	265,628	394,351
Central Region	28,851	48,181	81,583	127,009	197,365	267,915
Western Region	15,543	29,318	42,180	54,815	96,266	166,254
Southern Region	187,690	317,276	463,712	674,356	938,941	1,214,431
All India	**263,825**	**461,478**	**717,360**	**1,079,091**	**1,618,456**	**2,238,565**

Source: Southern Economist, November 1, 2008.

The region wise growth of SHGs of the country is explained in the Table 1.2.

The SHG position in the state of Odisha is explained in Table 1.3.

Table 1.3: SHGs formed in Odisha from Year 2001-02 to 2006-07 (Rs. In crores)

Year	No. of groups formed	No. of members (in lakhs)	Amount advanced	Amount of savings
2001-02	41475	5.57	15.34	13.54
2002-03	42782	5.42	39.12	22.02
2003-04	35735	4.39	113.20	35.46
2004-05	35418	4.50	175.39	31.16
2005-06	35373	4.15	143.13	68.44
2006-07	25762	3.13	79.71	72.46

Source: Economic Survey 2007-08, Government of Orissa.

Table 1.4 explains the growth of SHGs in the sample district Gajapati.

Table 1.4: Growth of SHGs in Gajapati district from year 2002-03 to 2007-08

Year	Cumulative number of SHGs	Total number of members	(Cumulative growth) Cumulative savings (Rs. In Lakhs)
2002-03	1258	17384	54.94
2003-04	1879	25853	111.28
2004-05	2711	35779	180.73
2005-06	2936	38437	231.98
2006-07	3229	41871	283.16
2007-08	4485	56502	413.93

Table 1.5 shows that maximum number of beneficiaries that is around 21.7% have received loan in the year 2006-2007, followed by 19% in the year n2005-2006 and 2007-2008, followed by 12% in the year 2004-2005. No beneficiaries have received loan in 1998-1999. This may be because the SHGs were formed in the sample district in the year 1999.8% of the beneficiaries have not yet received loan. Some of these beneficiaries belong to SHGs which are newly formed. Some of the beneficiaries belong to the SHGs which have applied for loan and are under processing.

Table 1.5: Loans granted to the SHGs beneficiaries during the year 1998-1999 to 2007-08 by the banks of Gajapati district

(Beneficiaries in number)

Sl. No.	Year	Loans granted to the beneficiaries (in number)	Loan amount to the beneficiaries (Rs.)
01.	1998-1999	0	0
02.	1999-2000	4	5080
03.	2000-2001	12	12200
04.	2001-2002	24	54440
05.	2002-2003	36	67990
06.	2003-2004	87	144009
07.	2004-2005	96	173808
08.	2005-2006	152	234195
09.	2006-2007	173	432508
10.	2007-2008	152	462962
11.	Not yet received	64	-
	Total	800	1587192

Source: Primary data collected from the questionnaires.

The loans taken by the beneficiaries from the SHGs are for both consumption and production purposes.

The SHG members can take loan from the group savings fund and also from the loan received from banks because of the bank linkages. Table-VI shows the purpose for which the SHG members have utilized the amounts they received from bank loans.

Table 1.6 explains the loans granted by various financial institutions viz. Regional Rural Banks (RRBs), Commercial Banks (CBs), and Co-operative Banks during different years to the SHG beneficiaries. Almost all the financial institutions of the district Gajapati have provided finance to the SHGs.

Table 1.6: Loan granted by different banks to the SHG beneficiaries during the year 1998-99 to 2007-08 in the sample district

(Loans in numbers)

Sl. No.	Banks Years	RRBs	CBs	Co-Operatives	Total
1	1998-99	0	0	0	0
2	1999-2000	3	1	0	4
3	2000-01	7	4	1	12
4	2001-02	16	6	2	24
5	2002-03	24	9	3	36
6	2003-04	56	24	7	87
7	2004-05	41	47	8	96
8	2005-06	64	84	4	152
9	2006-07	80	86	7	173
10	2007-08	80	64	8	152
11	Loans not yet received	-	-	-	64
	Total	371	325	40	800

Source: Primary data collected from the questionnaires.

From Table 1.7 it is clear that most of the loans taken by SHG members from SHG-Bank linkage are used up for production purpose. They utilize it for the income generating activities. They may take up individual income generating activities or sometimes group income generating activities.

Table 1.7: Purpose for which the bank loan amount was used by the SHG beneficiaries

(Beneficiaries in number)

Purpose of loan	Number of beneficiaries	Percentage
Consumption	272	34
Production	464	58
Loans not yet received	64	8
Total	800	100

Source: Primary data collected through questionnaires.

Table 1.8 indicates that a large number (around 72%) of micro enterprises started by the SHG members are individual enterprises. A few of them (around 28%) are group enterprises.

Table 1.8: The nature of micro-enterprises started by the SHG members

(Beneficiaries in number)

Type of enterprise	Number of beneficiaries
Individual	334
Group	130
Total	464

Source: Primary data collected from the questionnaires.

Table 1.9 shows the different enterprises taken up by the members of the SHGs.

Table 1.9: SHG Enterprises in the Sample District of Gajapati from 1998-99 to 2007-08

(Beneficiaries in numbers)

Type of the enterprises	Number of Beneficiaries
Incense sticks making	11
Tailoring and Embroidery	58
Animal Husbandry	65
Trading	81
Snacks and Papad and Badi making	92
Food processing	72
Mid day meal	23
Bakery	13
Poultry	35
Others	14
Total	464

Source: Primary data collected from questionnaire.

From Table 1.9, we find that most of the enterprises, that these members of the SHG of the sample district, are home based. They mostly do business using their domestic skills. The type of enterprise that is highest in number is snacks and papad making, followed by trading (mostly seasonal yields), followed by food processing, followed by animal husbandry, followed by tailoring and Embroidery, followed by poultry, followed by taking up mid day meal of schools in their areas, followed by others (viz. leafplate making, horticulture, broom stick making etc), followed by bakery units, followed by incense stick making.

CONCLUSIONS

The SHGs have helped the rural women to access financial support from the Banks and the Government by acting as intermediaries. There are a lot of entrepreneurial initiatives taken up by women in the rural areas, particularly by members of the SHGs. Most of the income generating activities that are taken up are individual and the group initiatives are very less. Most of the enterprises are home based micro enterprises.

REFERENCES

District Consultative Committee Meeting Reports, Lead Bank, Gajapati District from year 2003 to year 2008.

Gurumoorthy, T.R. "Self-Help Groups Empower Rural Women", *Kurukshetra*, Feb-2000.

Jain, Ritu, Kushawa, R.K. and Srivastava, A.K., 'Socio-Economic Impact Through Self-Help Groups', *Rural Empowerment*, Deep and Deep Publications, New Delhi, 2005.

Kumari, Y. Indira, and Rao B. Sambasiva, *Empowerment of women and Rural Development*, Serials Publications, New Delhi, 2005.

Narendra, Kumar I. and Komala, A.C., Performance Evaluation of SHGs in India, *Southern Economist*, November 1, 2008.

Nimala J. and Varadarajan Dhulasi Biruadha, "Empowerment of Women", *Kurukshetra*, March 2007.

Potential Linked Credit Plan 2008-09 for Gajapati, NABARD, Orissa Regional Office, Bhubaneswar, Orissa.

Role of Cooperative Banks in Financing Agricultural Credit in Orissa

*—Dr. Sudhansu Sekhar Nayak**

*—Dr. Rabi Narayan Misra***

INTRODUCTION

Agriculture is considered as the backbone of the Indian economy. More than 70 per cent of our total populations earn their livelihood from agriculture. From the very beginning, agriculture is contributing a major portion to our national income. In 1950-51, agriculture and allied activities contributed about 59 per cent of the total national income. Although the share of agriculture has been declining gradually with the growth of other sectors but the share still remained very high as compared to that of the developed countries of the world, for example, the share of agriculture has declined 54 per cent in 1960-61, 48 per cent in 1970-71, 40 per cent in 1980-81 and then to 26.1 per cent

* Lecturer in Commerce, Ramanarayan College, Dura-10, Ganjam (Orissa).

** Professor in MBA, S.M.I.T., Ankushpur, Berhampur, (Orissa).

in 2001-02, whereas in U.K. and U.S.A. agriculture contributes only 3 per cent to the national income of these countries only 3 per cent to the national income on these countries. In India over 2/3rds of our working population are engaged directly on agriculture and also similarly depend for their livelihood. According to an estimate, about 66 per cent o four working population are engaged in agriculture in comparison to that of 2 to 3 per cent in U.K. and U.S.A., 6 per cent in France, and 7 per cent in Australia. It has been estimated that about 60 per cent of household consumption is met by agricultural products. About 50 per cent of income generated in the manufacturing sector comes from the agro-based industries of India. Nearly 70 per cent of India's exports are originated from agricultural sector. The agriculture in India is totally backward at the time of independence. Due to the application of age-old and traditional techniques applied in agriculture, the productivity was very poor. During those days the land tenure system was mostly of *zamindari*, *Mahalwary* and *Ryotwari* type. The major production that is about 57 per cent of the total area was under Zamindari system, which paved the way for exploitation of peasants by the Zamindars. Since the introduction of economic planning in India, agricultural development has been receiving a special emphasis. It was only after 1965, i.e., from the mid-period of the Third Plan, special emphasis was laid on the development of the agricultural sector.

SCOPE AND OBJECTIVE OF THE STUDY

After the recommendation of the G.R. Gadgil Committee and the Renewal Credit Survey Committee, the Government of India emphasizes the co-operative agencies for development of rural economics. But in the present scenario, the cooperative banks are not able to meet the challenges of the commercial banks mostly after globalization. For the purpose of the study, we have taken the role of co-operative banks in financing agricultural credit in the state of Orissa. The Period of the study is limited only to six years, i.e. from 1998-99 to 2003-04 and only secondary data's are taken into consideration. So, all limitations of the secondary data are found in this study.

About Agricultural Credit

Agricultural credit is considered as one of the most basic input for conducting all agricultural development programmers. In India there is an immense need for proper agricultural credit as Indian farmers are very poor. From the very beginning the prime source of agricultural credit in India was money-lenders. After independence the government adopted the institutional credit approach through various agencies like cooperatives, commercial banks, regional rural banks, etc. to provide adequate credit to farmers, at a cheaper rate of interest.

TYPES OF AGRICULTURAL CREDIT

Considering the period and purpose of the credit requirement of the farmers of the country agricultural credit can be classified into three major types:

Short-term Credit

Farmers require credit to meet their short-term needs, i.e., purchasing seeds, fertilizers, paying wages to hired workers etc. for a period of less than 15 months.

Medium-term Credit

This type of credit includes credit requirement of farmers for medium period ranging between 15 months and five years and it is required for purchasing cattle, pumping sets, etc.

Long-term Credit

Farmers also require finance for a long period of more than five years just for the purpose of buying additional land or for making any permanent improvement on land, such as sinking of wells, reclamation of land, horticulture etc.

SOURCES OF AGRICULTURAL CREDIT

Agricultural credits are being advanced by different sources. Money-lenders, co-operative credit societies and Government mostly meet the short-term and medium term loan requirements of Indian farmers. But money-lenders, land development banks and the Government also meet the long-term loan requirements of the Indian farmers. Now a day, the long-term and short-term credit needs of these institutions are also being met by NABARD. Sources of agricultural credit can be broadly classified into institutional and non-institutional sources as follows.

INSTITUTIONAL SOURCES

The following are some of the important institutional sources of agricultural credit:

(i) **Co-operative Credit Societies:** the cheapest and the best source of rural credit is definitely the co-operative finance. In India the active primary agricultural credit societies (PACS) cover nearly 36 per cent of the total rural population of the country.

(ii) **Land Development Banks:** Land Development Banks are advancing long-term co-operative credit for 15-20 years to the farmers against the mortgage of their lands for its permanent improvement, purchasing agricultural implements and for repaying old debts

(iii) **Commercial Banks:** As per the recommendations of working group on Rural Banks the Regional Rural Banks (RRB) were established in 1975 for supplementing the commercial Banks and cooperatives in supplying rural credit. Since 1975 these RGB are advancing direct loans to small and marginal farmers, agricultural laborers and rural artisans etc. for productive purposes.

(iv) **Regional Rural Banks:** As per the recommendations of working group in Rural Banks the Regional Rural Banks (RRB) were established in 1975 for supplementing the commercial banks and cooperatives in supplying rural credit. Since 1975 these RRBS are advancing direct loans to small and marginal farmers, agricultural laborers and rural artisans etc. for productive purpose.

(v) **The Government:** Another important source of agricultural credit is the Government of our country. These loans are known as taccavi loans and are lend by the Government during emergency or distress like famine, flood, etc. The rate of interest charged against such loan is as low as 6 per cent.

NON-INSTITUTIONAL SOURCES

The important non-institutional source of agricultural credit are:

(i) **Money-lenders:** From the very beginning money-lenders have been advancing a major share of fram credit. Money-lenders are of two different types:

(a) professional money-lenders and

(b) agriculturist money-lenders. These money-lenders were supplying a major portion of agricultural credit.

(ii) **Traders and Commission Agents:** Traders and commission agents are also advancing loan to the agriculturalist for productive purposes before the maturity of crops and then force the farmers to sell their crops at very low prices and charge heavy commission. This type of loans is mostly advanced for cash crops.

(iii) **Relatives:** Cultivators are also normally borrowing fund from their own relatives at times of their crisis both in cash or kind. These loans are a kind of informal loans and carry no interest and are normally returned after harvest.

(iv) **Landlords:** Small as well as marginal formers and tenants are also taking loan from the landlords for meeting their financial requirements. This source has been following all the ill practices followed by money-lenders, traders, etc.

ANALYSIS

Orissa has a three-tier co-operative credit structure in rural areas for extending short and medium-term loans with Orissa State Co-operative Bank (OSCB) at the apex level with 8 branches, 17 Districts Central Co-operative Banks (DCCBs) at the district level with 323 branches and Primary Agricultural Co-operative Societies (PACs) at the base level with 2,726 branches. To provide long-term loans, there is a two-tier structure in the state with Orissa State Co-operative Agricultural Rural Development Bank (OSCARD) at the apex level and Co-operative Agricultural Rural Development Banks (card) at the base level. At present there are 50 primary CARD banks functioning mostly at the sub-divisional level to advance long-term agricultural credit for purposes like land shaping, purchase of tractors, power tillers, pump sets, etc. In the urban areas, 14 Urban Co-operative Banks, 687 Employees Credit Cooperative Societies etc. are functioning which provide loans to traders, salary and wage earners. The aggregate deposit and gross credit of cooperative banks during 2003-04 was Rs. 1761.25 Crore and Rs. 2,082.73 crore with a credit deposit ratio of 118.25 per cent. The analysis of the data is made under three heads:

(i) The year-wise position of cooperative societies in Orissa,

(ii) Sector-wise distribution of institutional credit flow in Orissa,

(iii) Targets and achievements of institutional credit flow in Orissa.

Year-wise Position of Agricultural Credit Cooperative Societies

The year-wise position indicating number of co-operative societies, their membership, working capital and loans advanced from the year 1998-99 to 2003-04 in Orissa have been indicated in Table 2.1.

Table 2.1 reveals that the member of cooperative societies as well as loans advanced are increasing year after year. Similarly, loans outstanding are also increasing. A lion's share of amount is locked up due to outstanding but the number of societies shows a fluctuating trend.

Sector-wise Distribution of Institutional Credit

The sector-wise distribution of institutional credit flow for the past six years (during 1998-99) in Orissa have been explained in Table 2.2

Table 2.2 shows that the sector-wise distribution of institutional credit flow in Orissa is increasing year after year. The total agricultural credit in Orissa was Rs. 605 crore in the year 1998-98 which has been increasing to Rs. 1,327 crore in the year 2003-04. Out of this, the crop loans was Rs. 1107 crore and the term loans was Rs. 220 crore in the year 2003-04.

Table 2.1: Year-wise Position of Agricultural credit co-operative societies in Orissa

Year	No. of Societies	Membership (In thousand)	Working capital (Rs. In Lakh)	Loans Advanced (Rs. In Lakh)	Loans Outstanding (Rs. In lakh)
1998-99	4,345	4,369	94,55	33,225	44,728
1999-2000	3,968	4,554	1,26,512	44,540	66,024
2000-01	4,202	4,638	1,38,856	51,852	78,966
2001-02	4,886	4,700	1,70,205	62,020	83,095
2002-03	4,702	4,659	1,91,293	69,069	94,501
2003-04	4,612	4,867	2,23,601	85,568	96,536

Source: Economic Survey, 2005-06, Government of Orissa, Bhubaneswar. P-ANX-47-48.

Table 2.2: Sector-Wise Distribution of Institutional Credit Flow in Orissa.

Sl. No.	Particulars	1998-99	1999-2000	2000-01	2001-02	2002-03	2003-04
i.	Crop Loans	455	523	633	754	870	1107
ii.	Term Loans	150	149	182	175	17	220
A	Minor Irrigation	26	17	30	21	22	26
B	Land Development	12	06	11	11	12	13
C	Farm Mechanisation	34	38	48	50	56	51
D	Plantation and Horticulture	08	11	14	13	10	37
E	Dairy Development	10	10	17	16	12	11
F	Poultry	04	05	08	09	09	09
G	Sheep/Goat/Piggery	10	12	13	15	12	17
H	Fisheries	08	07	09	09	14	12
I	Forestry/Wasteland Dev.	01	02	03	04	03	03
J	Storage and Market Yard	02	05	07	08	08	09
K	Others	35	37	23	19	18	31
	Total Agricultural credit	**605**	**672**	**816**	**929**	**1,047**	**1,327**

Source: Orissa state focus paper, 2002 and 2005, NABARD, Orissa, Regional office, Bhubaneswar.

Targets and Achievement of institutional Credit

The targets and achievements of institutional credit flow in Orissa from the year 1998-99 to 2003-04 were presented in Table 2.3.

Table 2.3: Targets and Achievements of Institutional Credit Flow in Orissa

Sl. No.	Particulars	1998-99	1999-2000	2000-01	2001-02	2002-03	2003-04
I	*Crop Loans:*						
	Targets	393	525	663	750	904	974
	Achievements	455	523	633	754	870	1107
	% Achieved	116	100	96	100	96	114
II	*Term Loans:*						
	Targets	266	283	182	379	409	420
	Achievements	150	149	182	175	177	220
	% Achieved	56	53	55	46	43	52
III	*Total Agricultural* Credit:						
	Targets	393	660	808	996	1129	1394
	Achievements	605	672	816	929	1047	1327
	% Achieved	92	83	82	82	80	95

Source: Orissa state focus paper, 2002 and 2005, *NABARD, Bhubaneswar, Orissa..*

Table 2.3 shows that in almost all the years starting from 1998-99 the percentage of targets were achieved. In the year 2003-04, 95 per cent of targets were achieved as against 92 per cent of targets were achieved in the year 1998-99 for total agricultural credit in Orissa.

SUGGESTIONS

For the effective modernization of agricultural sector and also to stimulate its growth pattern a broad based and simplified rural accredit structure is very much desired and important. Thus, in order to remove limitations and problems of agricultural credit the following measures may be suggested:

(1) Co-operative credit societies should be organized to make it efficient and purposeful for delivering the best in terms of rural credit.

(2) To monitor the taccavi loan offered by the Government in a serious manner.

(3) Middlemen existing between credit agencies and borrowers should be criminated.

(4) Reserve Bank of India should arrange sufficient funds so that long-term loans can be advanced to the formers.

(5) Power and activities of the Mahajans and money-lenders should be checked so as to declare an end to the exploitation of farmers.

(6) The government should introduce the credit guarantee scheme so as to provide guarantee on behalf of the farmers for getting loans.

(7) The banks should adopt procedural simplification for credit delivery through rationalization of its working pattern.

(8) The government should issue Kissan credit cards to the farmers to draw cash for their production needs on the basis of the model scheme prepared by NABARD.

(9) Credit should also monitor over the actual utilization of loans by developing an effective supervisory mechanism.

(10) In order to check the fraud practices adopted by the farmer, a credit card should be issued against each farmer, which will show the details about the loans taken by them from different agencies.

CONCLUSION

From the above analysis it has been revealed that the extent of agricultural credit is very much inadequate and the private non-institutional sources still remained very important in supplying credit to the farmers. Further, the major problem of institutional credit faced by lending institutions, particularly the cooperatives, is the unsatisfactory huge level of over dues ranging between 40 to 47 per cent. This has resulted a bad health to the institutional credit and thus these lending institutions will not be able to advance more credit for meeting the growing needs of our farmers. In spite of that, these institutional sources now-a-days are advancing more than 60 per cent of the required short-term production credit to the farmers, but the major portion of these credits is being appropriated by the 30 per cent of the middle and affluent farmers. In spite of drastic change in banking sector after globalization, the role of cooperatives cannot be ignored. It has played lion's share in the development of rural economy of the State of Orissa. More and more persons are coming under the fold of cooperatives in the rural area. Central and State Governments play crucial role in rural credit through introduction of sponsored schemes, priority sector lending, subsidy linked programmers, etc. The farmers and entrepreneurs must take advantage of it. Last but not least, it warrants concerted efforts from government and non-government organizations, and also from every responsible citizen, researcher and educationist to educate the people about the advantage of institutional finance, commercialization in farming practices, schemes for agricultural and allied activities and moreover to maintain a sustainable business relation with financing banks.

Role of Financial Institutions in Economic Development of Orissa

—*Prof. R.P. Sarma*

Finance is the crucial factor for economic development. When financial institutions growing in a region it accelerates economic development and the *vice versa* is also true, that is when economy grows the financial institutions also grow to provide, long-term, short-term and working capital to the industrial as well as to the agricultural sector. It is the responsibility of the state to provide suitable environment to encourage the financial institutions.

Orissa being an under developed state the banking institutions are reluctant to open brunches in the state and even if there is expansion of the branches it mainly concentrate on the urban areas and the industrial centres. They always reluctant to provide and invest funds in the rural sector mainly because of two important factors: (1) one is the rural people are not yet

* Professor Economics (Rtd.), Berhampur University, Orissa.

acquainted with the banking system, (2) two, the commercial banks find it difficult to recover loan from the rural and agricultural sector hence prefer to invest in non-agricultural sector.

There are four types of financial institutions that provide finance for the development of the State through different schemes of State as well as Central Government:

(1) Commercial banks,

(2) Regional Rural Banks,

(3) Co-operative banks and

(4) other capital banks that provide long-term funds which are mainly of all India financial organizations.

Of the four types of financial institutions the commercial banks mainly provide funds to the urban and industrial sector while the RRBs and the Co-operatives provide credit to the rural and agricultural sector. The all India capital market institutions prove funds for both rural and urban industrial projects sponsored by State and Central government.

COMMERCIAL BANKS

The commercial banks again can be classified into two categories: (1) public sector commercial banks and (2) commercial banks in the private sector. At the end of the year 2003-04 there were total 2242 branches of this the private sector commercial banks have 16 branches. In both numbers of branches as well as in mobilization deposits the public sector banks are far ahead of the public banks.

Table 3.1 shows the number of branches of the commercial banks along with the deposit mobilisation and advancement of credit. The trend of growth of deposits and credit is shown in Fig. 3.1.

Table 3.1: Growth of Deposits and Credit of the Commercial Banks in Orissa

Year	No. of Branches	Deposit Rs. in crores	Credit Rs.in crores	Credit deposit ratio
1990-91	2084	2,637	2,126	80.59
1995-96	2154	6,006	3,292	54.81
1999-00	2219	12,733	5,062	39.75
2001-02	2224	18,689	8,527	45.63
2002-03	2232	20,348	10,431	51.26
2003-04	2242	23,360	13,391	57.32

Source: Economic Survey (Orissa) 2000-01 and 2003-04.

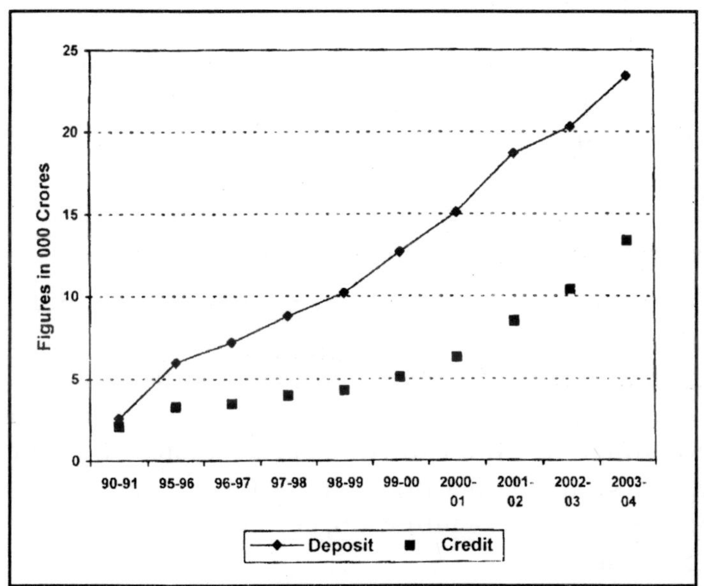

Fig. 3.1: Growth of Deposits and Credit of Commercial Banks

The growth rate of the deposits in 1990s increased almost five times, at average annual growth rate of 1.12 per cent, but in the early 21st century form 2000-2004 the annual growth rate registered 2.66 per cent. Advancement of credit was very slow. The credit-deposit ratio was at the highest rate of 80.59 per cent but at the end of the 1990s reduced to 39.75 per cent which recovered but at the end of the 2003-04 it is only 57.32 per cent. There are 16 branches of private commercial banks in the state and their credit-deposit rate is very low in comparison to the public sector commercial banks. The private banks have credit ratio of 35.39 per cent in 2003-04 as against the public sector banks with ratio of 58.17 per cent in the same year.

Out of the total of Rs. 11,321 crores advances to all the sectors in Orissa in the year 2003-04 by the public sector banks advances to agricultural sector is 10.36 per cent. The highest portion of funds is invested in service sector followed by funds to the state government. The advance to the small industries is not significant as about 8 per cent advances gone to the small scale industries sector. The respective figures for the year 2003-04 are show in Table 3.2.

The private sector commercial banks provided higher proportion of their credit to the agricultural sector, which was 18.69 per cent in 2003-04. Both the category of commercial banks advanced higher percentage of funds to the service sector; but the private sector banks provided 24.04 per cent to the service sector as against 36 per cent by the public sector banks.

Table 3.2: Advances to Different Sectors, 2003-04

Sector	Loan Advanced Rs. in Crores	Per cent
Services	4,115	36.35
Government	3225	28.48
Others	1,235	10.91
Agriculture	1,173	10.36
Small Industries	912	8.06
ST and SC	661	5.84
Total	11,321	100

Source: Economic Survey (Orissa) 2003-04.

REGIONAL RURAL BANKS

The Regional Rural Banks (RRB) were set up in the year 1975 with exclusive objective of providing funds to agriculture and other economic activities in the rural sector. It started with five RRBs initially and presently there are 196 RRBs in 23 states of India. RRB is a joint effort by Central, State government and a sponsoring commercial bank. The authorized share capital is one crore shared in proportion of 50 :25 :35 respectively by Centre, State and sponsoring bank.

There are nine RRBs in Orissa with 832 branches sponsored by five commercial banks, namely, Andhra Bank, UCo Bank, State Bank of India, Bank of India and Indian Overseas Bank. During the period of seven years from 1994 to 2000 the number of branches increased from 773 to 832 with an annual growth rate of 5.9 per cent but there after the branch expansion remained stable. The growth of deposits and advancement of credit was higher to the growth rate of branches, especially during the period of 2000 to 2004. During this period there was 128.50 per cent increase in advancement of credit in four years. The Credit-Deposit ratio however declined from 74.29 in 1994 to 58.83 per cent in 2004. The figures of deposit and credit are presented in Table 3.3.

The RRBs are designed for the expansion of credit to the agricultural sector but the highest proportion of credit gone to the service sector which constituted as high as 46.44 per cent. The agricultural sector received 25.23 per cent of the total disbursement of credit of the RRBs in the year 2004 which of course higher to the disbursement of credit to the agriculture sector by the commercial banks.

Table 3.3: Growth of Deposits and Credit of RRBs in Orissa

Year	No of Branches	Deposits Rs. Crores	Credit Rs. Crores	C-D Ratio
1994	773	350	260	74.29
1996	763	575	365	63.48
1998	763	927	522	56.42
2000	823	1505	758	50.37
2002	832	2212	1024	46.29
2003	832	2500	1409	65.36
2004	832	2944	1732	58.83

Source: Economic Survey (Orissa), 2000-01 and 2003-04.

CO-OPERATIVE BANKS

The state has three tier co-operative credit structures to provide short- and medium-term loans to the rural sector by these co-operative organizations:

1. The Orissa State Co-operative Bank (OSEB) - eight branches.

2. District Central Co-operative Banks (DCCB) - 323 branches.
3. Primary Agricultural Co-operative Societies, (PACS) - 2726 which includes 218 Large Size Adivasi Multipurpose Societies (LAMPS) and six Farmers' Service Societies (FSS).
4. Orissa State Co-operative Agricultural Rural Development Bank (OSCARD) at apex level.
5. Co-operative Agricultural Rural Development (CARD) 50 branches.
6. Urban Co-operative Banks, 14 in number.

The co-operative credit societies advanced total loan of Rs. 89.31 crores to the rural sector in the year 1990-91 which increased to a huge amount of Rs. 1710.05 crores by the year 2002-03. The annual growth rate which was 30.02 per cent in the early 1990s came down to 13.38 per cent by the year 2002-03. In the year 2001-02 the growth was found negative because of lower disbursement of loan to the non-agricultural sector that year.

It is found that the co-operative societies provided more loans to the non-agricultural sector in the state than the agricultural sector; this has been the trend after the year 1994-95. In the year 1990-91 the loans to the non-agricultural sector formed 60.73 per cent which increased to 63.72 per cent by the year 2002-03. Co-operative credit to the agricultural and non-agricultural sectors in the rural areas of the state from the year 1990-91 to 2002-03 in selected years is presented in Table 3.4.

Table 3.4: Advance of Co-operative Loans in Orissa

Year	Agri. Rs. Crores	Non-Agri Rs. Crores	Total	Growth
1990-91	35.07	54.24	89.31	
1994-95	122.86	80.85	203.71	30.02
1999-00	445.40	666.98	1112.38	89.21
2000-01	518.52	857.02	1375.54	23.66
2001-02	620.20	730.50	1350.74	-1.80
2002-03	620.69	1089.36	1710.05	13.38

Source: Economic Survey (Orissa), 2000-01 and 2003-04.

NON-BANKING ORGANISATIONS

There is several non-banking organizations of all India, provided finance to the different sectors in Orissa and helped the State to accelerate economic growth. The long-term and medium-term investments made by the seven organisations by the end of 2002-03 is shown in Table 3.5. The first two in the table OSFC and ORHDC are the state financial institutions while the other five are the national organisations. The state organisations invested Rs. 577.32 crores while the national organizations invested Rs. 3253.71.38 crores in the State.

The highest investor is the LIC of India which has total investment of Rs. 1726.60 crores which forms 45.08 per cent of all the investors in the State together. But the LIC is mainly invests in government securities which forms 87 per cent of its totals investment in the state. The HUDCO, the national housing development organization is second in position in investment of Rs. 1081.18 crores followed by the

NABARD which aids mainly to development of agriculture and rural sector of Rs. 308.38 crores.

Table 3.5: Investment by the National and State Financial Organisation up to 2002-03

State and All-India Organisations	Investment Rs. Crores
Orissa SFC	10.47
Orissa RHDC	566.85
Total	577.32
LIC	1726.60
IDBI	108.06
SIDBI	29.49
NABARD	308.38
HUDCO	1081.18
Grant Total	**3831.03**

Source: Economic Survey (Orissa), 2000-01 and 2003-04.

The financial institutions of Commercial Banks, RRBs and Co-operative Societies together extended loan of Rs. 13,550 crores in the state in the year 2003 of which the Commercial Banks are in the first position who extended Rs. 10,431 crores which formed 76.98 per cent of the total credit. The co-operative societies are in the second position and the RRBs in the third. The dominance of Commercial Banks can be visualized from the pie diagram presented in Fig. 3.2.

CONCLUSION

In the year 2002-03 the NSDP of Orissa at factor cost was Rs. 38,241 crores in current prices and the financing of the banking institutions of Rs.13,550

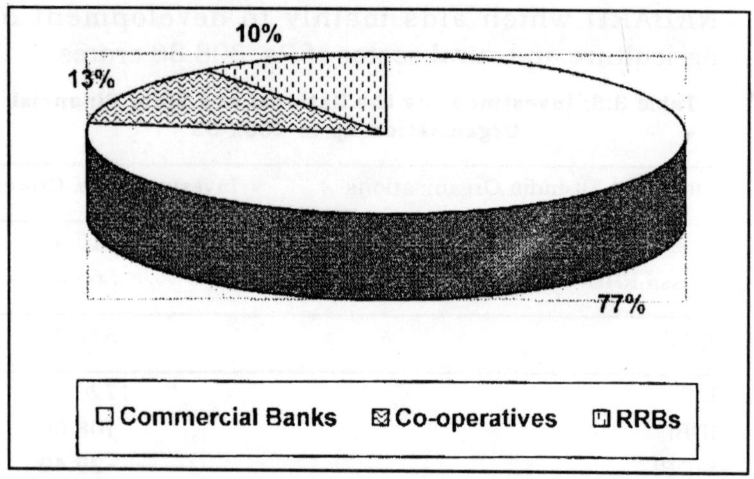

Fig. 3.2: Participation of Financial Institutions in Extension of Credit in Orissa-2003

crores formed 35.43 of the NSDP. Investment of the non-banking institutions are not included in this calculation since their figures are cumulative figures instead of annual figures. Between 2002 and 2003 the total credit extended to the state by the banking institutions increased from Rs. 10,903 crores to Rs. 13,550 a growth rate of 24.29 per cent which increased the NSDP of Orissa by 4.52 per cent.

The growth of NSDP at factor cost in constant prices of 1993-94 the annual growth rate from 2001-02 to 2002-03 was negative to the extent of 1.05. If the state aspires to reach 10 per cent annual growth there would be at least the double the credit flow to the state presently (2002-03) of Rs.13,550 crores to about Rs. 27 thousand crores. The state government's plan expenditure was Rs.2,474 crores in the year 2002-03. The total of credit extended by the banking sector and the Government's plan expenditure comes to Rs. 16,024 crores; this shows a deficit of Rs.10,976 crores to aspiring 10 per cent growth rate of the NSDP expenditure of Rs. 27 thousand crores.

REFERENCES

Government of Orissa, *Economic Survey 2000-01*, Bhubaneswar

Government of Orissa, *Economic Survey 2004-05*, Bhubaneswar

Government of Orissa, *Statistical Abstract of Orissa – 2005*, Bhubaneswar

Government of Orissa, *Statistical Outline of Orissa, 1999 and 2003*, Bhubaneswar.

4 Micro Finance in India

*—Prof. Rabi Narayana Mishra**

*—Dr. Satyabrat Dash***

DEFINITION

Micro-finance refers to small savings, credit and insurance services extended to socially and economically disadvantaged segments of society. In Indian context terms like "small and marginal farmers", "rural artisans" and "economically weaker sections" have been used to broadly define micro-finance customers. The recent Task Force on Micro Finance has defined it as "provision of thrift, credit and other financial services and products of very small amounts to the poor in rural, semi urban or urban areas, for enabling them to raise their income levels and improve living standards". At present, a large part of micro-finance activity is confined to credit only. Women constitute a vast majority of users of micro-credit and savings services.

* Professor, P.G. Centre for Management Studies, S.M.I.T., Berhampur, India

** Lecturer, P.G. Centre for Management Studies, S.M.I.T., Berhampur, India.

DEMAND OF MICRO FINANCE SERVICES IN INDIA

Due to its large size and population of around 1000 million, India's GDP ranks among the top 15 economies of the world. However, around 300 million people or about 60 million households, are living below the poverty line. It is further estimated that of these households, only about 20 per cent have access to credit from the formal sector. Additionally, the segment of the rural population above the poverty line but not rich enough to be of interest to the formal financial institutions also does not have good access to the formal financial intermediary services, including savings services. A group of micro-finance practitioners estimated the annualized credit usage of all poor families (rural and urban) at over Rs 45,000 crores, of which some 80 per cent is met by informal sources. This figure has been extrapolated using the numbers of rural and urban poor households and their average annual credit usage (Rs 6,000 and Rs 9,000 pa respectively) assessed through various micro studies.

Credit on reasonable terms to the poor can bring about a significant reduction in poverty. It is with this hypothesis; micro credit assumes significance in the Indian context. With about 60 million households below or just above the austerely defined poverty line and with more than 80 per cent unable to access credit at reasonable rates, it is obvious that there are certain issues and problems, which have prevented the reach of micro-finance to the needy. With globalisation and liberalization of the economy, opportunities for the unskilled and the illiterate are not increasing fast enough, as compared to the rest of the economy. This is leading to a lopsided growth in the economy thus increasing the gap between the haves and have-nots. It is in this context, the institutions involved in micro-finance have a significant role to play to reduce this disparity and lead to more equitable growth.

DEMANDS FOR CREDIT

In terms of demand for micro-credit, there are three segments: At the very bottom in terms of income and assets, and most numerous, are those who are landless and are engaged in agricultural work on a seasonal basis, and manual laborers in forestry, mining, household industries, construction and transport. This segment requires, first and foremost, consumption credit during those months when they do not get labour work, and for contingencies such as illness. They also need credit for acquiring small productive assets, such as livestock, using which they can generate additional income. The next market segment is small and marginal farmers and rural artisans, weavers and those self-employed in the urban informal sector as hawkers, vendors, and workers in household micro enterprises. This segment mainly needs credit for working capital, a small part of which also serves consumption needs. In rural areas, one of the main uses of working capital is for crop production. This segment also needs term credit for acquiring additional productive assets, such as irrigation pump sets, bore wells and livestock in case of farmers, and equipment (looms, machinery) and work sheds in case of non-farm workers. This market segment also largely comprises the poor but not the poorest.

The third market segment is of small and medium farmers who have gone in for commercial crops such as surplus paddy and wheat, cotton, groundnut, and others engaged in dairying, poultry, fishery, etc. Among non-farm activities, this segment includes those in villages and slums, engaged in processing or manufacturing activity, running provision stores, repair workshops, tea shops, and various service enterprises. These persons are not always poor, though they live barely above the poverty line and also suffer from inadequate access to formal credit.

One market segment, which is of great importance to micro-credit, is women. The 1991 Census figures reveal that out of total 2.81 million marginal workers, 2.54 million were women and their further break-up shows that out of a total of 2.67 million rural marginal workers, 2.44 million were females. Further, many more women were willing to work. This has been corroborated by the results of a survey done by the National Sample Survey Organization (NSSO), 43rd round, which has revealed that there is a vide variety of work which rural women combine with household work.

In the NSSO survey it has also been estimated that a large percentage of rural women in the age group of 15 years and above, who are usually engaged in household as dairy (9.5 per cent), poultry (3 per cent), cattle rearing, spinning and weaving (3.4 per cent), tailoring (6.1 per cent) and manufacturing of wood and cane products etc. Amongst the women surveyed, 27.5 per cent rural women were seeking regular full-time work, and 65.3 per cent were seeking part-time work. To start or to carry on such work, 53.6 per cent women wanted initial finance on easy terms, and 22.2 per cent wanted working capital facilities, as can be seen from Table 4.1 below.

Table 4.1: Assistance required (by woman marginal workers seeking or available for work at their household premises)

Assistance Required (by woman marginal workers seeking or available for work at their household premises)	Percent of woman seeking assistance
No assistance	2.1
Initial finance on easy terms	53.6
Working capital facilities	22.2
Raw materials availability	4.6
Marketing	1.7
Training	10.5
Accommodation	0.4
Other assistance	4.9
Total	100.00

DEMAND FOR SAVINGS AND INSURANCE SERVICES

The demand for savings services is ever higher than for credit. Studies of rural households in various states in India show that the poor, particularly women, are looking for a way to save small amounts whenever they can. The irregularity of cash flows and the small amounts available for savings at one time, deter them from using formal channels such as banks. In urban areas also this is true, in spite of better banking facilities, as shown by the experience of the SEWA Bank, Ahmedabad. The poor want to save for various reasons – as a cushion against contingencies like illness, calamities, death in the family, etc., as a source of equity or margin to take loans; and finally, as a liquid asset. The safety of savings is of higher concern than interest rates. The demand for savings services is high in rural areas as well, as can be seen from a recent study of women's savings and credit movement in Andhra Pradesh. Almost all women's groups in their early years begin with regular savings and their savings exceed the loans they give from their funds. Of course, part of this lower demand for credit is the inadequate absorption capacity of women, which comes from long years of exclusion from the economic sphere outside their homes. The demand for insurance services, though not very well articulated, is also substantial. This comes from the fact that not only incomes of micro-finance customers low, but are also highly variable. Insurance by the poor is needed for assets such as livestock and pump sets, for shelter. Crop insurance could be very useful to the rural poor. Finally, insurance against illness, disability and death would also reduce the shocks caused by such contingencies, which lead the poor into taking loans at such times at high interest.

SUPPLY OF MICRO-FINANCE SERVICES

Reserve Bank of India data show that informal sources provide a significant part of the total credit needs of the rural population. The magnitude of the dependence of the rural poor on informal sources of credit can be observed from the findings of the All-India Debt and Investment Survey, 1992, which shows that the share of the non-institutional agencies (informal sector) in the outstanding cash dues of the rural households was 36 per cent. However, the dependence of rural households on such informal sources had reduced of their total outstanding dues steadily form 83.7 per cent in 1961 to 36 per cent in 1991. This is shown in Table 4.2 below:

Table 4.2: The dependence of rural households (Cultivators Non-Cultivators)

Year	Cultivators	Non-Cultivators	All
1961	81.6	89.5	83.7
1971	60.3	89.2	70.8
1981	36.8	63.3	38.8
1991	33.7	44.7	36.0

Among formal institutional sources, banks and co-operatives provided credit support to almost 56 per cent of the rural households, while professional and agricultural money lenders were providing credit to almost one sixth of the rural households. The details by source are given in Table 4.3 below:

Table 4.3: Sources of Credit for Rural Households, 1991

Credit Agency	% of Rural Household
Government etc	6.1
Cooperative Society	21.6
Commercial Banks and RRBs	33.7
Insurance	0.3
Provident Fund	0.7
Other Institutional Sources	1.6
All Institutional Agencies	64.0
Landlord	4.0
Agricultural Money-lenders	7.0
Professional Money-lenders	10.5
Relatives and Friends	5.5
Others	9.0
All Non-institutional Agencies	36.0
All Agencies	100.0

Though the overall share of institutional credit for rural households has gone up steadily, households in the lower asset groups were more dependent on the non-institutional credit agencies. The share of debt from the non-institutional credit agencies was 58 per cent in the case of lowest asset group of "less than Rs. 5,000" as against a low of 19 per cent in the highest asset group of "Rs 2.5 lakh and above".

SHARE OF DEBT FROM INSTITUTIONAL AND NON-INSTITUTIONAL SOURCES, BY ASSET HOLDINGS OF HOUSEHOLDS

Over the decades following India's independence in 1947, Government of India (GOI) has made concerted efforts to provide micro-finance to the rural poor through the formal financial sector namely the co-operatives. However, the limited success of the co-operatives in the mid fifties to the sixties forged the need for nationalization of Commercial Banks (CB) in 1971 and the establishment of a large network to reach every village, and every segment of the population. In the mid-1970s, Regional Rural Banks (RRB) were also established to continue further the outreach of the banking sector in reaching the rural poor. All these programs were supported by a policy of mandated credit programs for the low-income households that were supported by the Integrated Rural Development Program (IRDP), launched in 1980. The IRDP was designed to provide a mix of subsidy from the government and credit from the banking system to enable the asset acquisition of the poor.

As a result of these programs, India has one of the largest banking networks in the world with close to

50,000 CB outlets; 14,420 RRBs; and 90,000 primary agricultural co-operative societies. Close to 43 per cent of the CB, and RRB branches are located in the rural areas. Even more impressive is the fact that, there is a financial intermediary branch for every 15,000 households, and a co-operative in every village.

Due to the extensive expansion of the banking network and emphasis on lending to small borrowers, there have been a lot of small loans by banks. In terms of amount, this was 13.2 per cent of the total credit outstanding from commercial banks and RRBs. As per RBI data for March 1994, the number of accounts below Rs 25,000 was 5.6 million, or 93.6 per cent of total loan accounts, with 18.6 per cent of the outstanding amount. Of these, accounts with outstanding below Rs 7500 comprised 80.5 per cent of the number of accounts and 49.5 per cent of amount outstanding. In terms of purpose, 45.8 per cent of amount was for small agricultural loans, 20.2 per cent for industry and 18.8 per cent for trade and services.

By March 1997, the number of small borrower accounts with a credit limit below Rs 25,000 had come down by as many 0.6 million accounts to 5.0 million, or 90.1 per cent of the outstanding loan accounts. This decline in number of accounts clearly shows the post liberalization trend, with banks concentrating their efforts on larger loans and becoming ever more reluctant to extend credit to small borrowers.

While banks have been engaged in financing small borrowers, the manner in which this is being done can hardly be called micro-finance. The procedures are cumbersome, the staff unfriendly and the transaction costs high. Repeat loans, except for crop production, are rare, even for borrowers who have repaid fully. Furthermore, even though the many of the loans extended to the poor by the public sector financial institutions are subsidized, their ultimate cost to the borrowers is high: factoring in out-of-pocket costs, payments to middle men, wage and business loss due to time spent in getting the loan approved. Effectively, the total cost of funds to the borrower ranges between 22-30 per cent as against the 12-14 per cent nominal lending rates specified for commercial bank loans below Rs 200,000. All this results in low repayment rates, leading to a various cycle of non-availability and nor-repayment.

SUPPLY OF SAVINGS AND INSURANCE SERVICES

In the case of savings services, again while banks have provided access to a large number of small depositors, the demand is nowhere near being met, particularly for small, frequent "recurring" deposits. Hence the poor turn to other means such as chits, bishis and savings mobilization companies like Peerless and Sahara. Many such companies are fly-by night and as a result, the poor lose their money. The RBI has tightened up deposit taking activity since 1997, but this has, perversely, also led to legitimate MFIs being not allowed to take deposits and thus provide savings services to the poor. Transaction costs of savings in formal institutions were as high as 10 per cent for the rural poor, because of small average transaction size and distance of the bank form villages.

The supply of insurance services to the poor has been increased substantially over the 1990s, and there are a large number of low premium schemes covering them against death, accidents, natural calamities, and loss of assets due to fire, theft, etc. However, the usage is limited by low awareness among the poor. Crop and livestock insurance, however, are quite expensive and their reach to the poor is negligible. Livestock and asset insurance was extended top the poor along with the IRDP subsidized loans, and thus remained scheme driven, with little awareness among the customers.

MICRO-FINANCE INSTITUTIONAL STRUCTURE

The different organizations in this field can be classified as “Mainstream” and “Alternative” Micro-Finance Institutions (MFI).

Mainstream Micro-finance Institutions

National Agricultural Bank for Rural Development (NABARD), Small Industries Development Bank of India (SIDBI), Housing Development Finance Corporation (HDFC), Commercial Banks, Regional Rural Banks (RRBs), the credit co-operative societies etc. are some of the mainstream financial institutions involved in extending micro-finance.

Alternative Micro Finance Institutions

These are the institutions, which have come up to fill the gap between the demand and supply for micro-finance. MFIs were recently defined by the Task Force as “those which provide thrift, credit and other financial services and products of very small amounts, mainly to the poor, in rural, semi-urban areas for enabling them to raise their income level and improve living standards." The MFIs can broadly be classified as:

- NGOs, which are mainly engaged in promoting self-help groups (SHGs) and their federations at a cluster level, and linking SHGs with banks, under the NABARD scheme.
- NGOs directly lending to borrowers, who are either organized into SHGs or into Grameen Bank style groups and centres. These NGOs borrow bulk funds from RMK, SIDBI, FWWB and various donors.
- MFIs which are specifically organized as cooperatives, such as the SEWA Bank and various Mutually Aided Cooperative Thrift and Credit Societies (MACTS) in AP.
- MFIs, which are organized as non-banking finance companies, such as BASIX, CFTS, Mirzapur and SHARE Microfin Ltd.

Some of the leading alternative micro-finance institutions in this segment are SEWA Bank in Gujarat, which also runs federations of SHGs in nine districts; ASSEFA and its Sarva Jana Seva Kosh Ltd, the and ASA in Tamil Nadu: SHARE, BASIX, CARE and MACTs in AP promoted among others by the Cooperative Development Foundation (CDF); MYRADA in Karnataka, which has promoted Sanghamitra, a company of its village savings and credit sanhas; PRADAN which has established a large number of SHGs and federated them under Damodar in Bihar, Sakhi Samiti in Rajasthan and the Kalanjiams in Tamil Nadu (the last now run by DHAN Foundation); ADITHI in Bihar has established. Nari Nidhi, a federation of women's groups; PREM in Orissa has done the same through the Utkal Mahila Sanchay O Bikas; the Rashtriya Gramin Vikas Nidhi which runs credit and savings programs in Assam and Orissa, on the lines of the Grameen Bank, Bangladesh, as does SHARE in AP, ASA in Tamil Nadu and RDO in Manipur.

THE PROBLEMS ASSOCIATED WITH MAINSTREAM MFIs

To enable the reach of micro-finance services to the needy, the problems associated with the legal, regulatory, organizational systems and the attitudes should be addressed to and the desired changes brought in these, to make them more effective.

The mainstream financial institutions are flush with funds and have access to enormous amounts of low cost savings deposits. Indeed, the poorer the region, the lower the credit deposit ratio-most of the eastern UP, Bihar, Orissa and the North-East have Credit Deposit ratios of 20-30 per cent. Thus while banks are physically present in rural areas and offer concessional interest rates, rural producers are not able to access, with the result that the rest of the deposits are finding their way into the financial sector. Some of the main reasons for the above are:

Borrower Unfriendly Products and Procedures

With a majority of the customers being illiterate, and a majority of them needing consumption loans and a majority of them requiring high documentation and collateral security, the products are not reaching the rural poor.

Inflexibility and Delay

The rigid systems and procedures result in lot of time delay for the borrowers and de-motivate them to take further loans.

High Transaction Costs, both Legitimate and Illegal

Although the interest rate offered to the borrowers is regulated, the transaction costs in terms of the number of trips to be made the documents to be furnished etc. plus the illegal charges to be paid result in increasing the cost of borrowing. Thus, making it less attractive to the borrowers.

Social Obligation and not a Business Opportunity

Micro-finance has historically been seen as a social obligation rather than a potential business opportunity.

Financing to Alternative MFIs

NABARD Act does not permit them to refinance any private sector FI and do any direct financing (NABARD's direct lending to micro-finance NGOs so far has been out of donor funds), similarly SIDBI Act restricts it from extending loans to the agricultural and allied sectors, whereas many of the members of the self-help groups are engaged in such activities.

Legal and Regulatory Framework

- The policy-makers feel that farmers and poor people need low interest and subsidized credit.

Thereby we have regulated interest regime for the loans up to Rs 25,000 and Rs 2,00,000 with an interest cap of 12 per cent and 13.5 per cent respectively. They believe that poor cannot save, they are unwilling to repay the loans, and the administrative costs of servicing them are high.

- Also small loans have been used as a tool for disbursing political patronage, undermining the norm that loans must be repaid. Thus the mainstream institutions feel that these loans are risky, difficult to serve and have a low or negative net spread.
- The Regional Rural Banks Act does not permit any private share holding in any RRBs, and the Cooperative Act of all states do not permit district level co-operative banks to be set up except by the state government. The result of these two laws together is that rural credit has been a monopoly of state owned institutions.

PROBLEMS FOR ALTERNATIVE MICRO-FINANCE INSTITUTIONS

The main aim with which the alternative MFIs have come up is to bridge the increasing gap between the demand and supply. A vast majority of them set up as NGOs for getting access to funds as, the existing practices of mainstream financing institutions such as SIDBI and NABARD and even of the institutions specially funding alternatives, such RMK and FWWB, is to fund only NGOs, or NGO promoted SHGs. As a result, the largest incentive to enter such services remains through the non-profit route. The alternative finance institutions also have not been fully successful in reaching the needy. There are many reasons for this:

- Financial problems leading to setting up of inappropriate legal structures,
- Lack of commercial orientation,
- Lack of proper governance and accountability
- Isolated and scattered.

Inappropriate Legal Forms

NGOs invented micro-finance but NGOs are not the best type of agencies to carry out micro-finance on a long-term sustainable basis. If an MFI opts to become an NGO, it has the following problems:

- The major sources of funds of NGOs are grants, which are very limited.
- If the NGOs earn a substantial part of their income from lending activity, they violate Section 11(4) of the Income-tax Act and can lose their charitable status under Section 12.
- Moreover, NGOs do not have the appropriate financial structure for carrying out micro-finance activities. NGOs being registered as societies or trusts do not have any equity capital and can never be "capital adequate".

The other alternative for an MFI is to become ac cooperative or a company. As in the long-run, the primary source of lending funds for MFIs is deposits, till that stage, the MFI has to rely on borrowings. To be able to attract borrowings, the MFI has to have equity capital. Thus, it is only possible to establish a financially sustainable MFI either as a cooperative or as a company.

In most states, with exception of Andhra Pradesh, Maharashtra, and Gujarat, cooperatives are politicized and State controlled and thus not an appropriate form of incorporation of ran MFI. That leaves an MFI with the choice to be incorporated as a company and then become an NBFC or a Bank. The latter requires a license and a minimum start up equity of Rs 100 crores, which is very difficult for an MFI to mobilize. The concept of Local Area Bank, with a lower start up capital of Rs 5 crores, has not yet been operationalized by the government. If an MFI opts to become an NBFC, it has the following problems.

- The minimum entry-level capital requirements are Rs. 2 Crores, w.e.f. April 1999.
- It is difficult to mobilize any borrowings from Indian Financial Institutions due to the negative image of NBFCs in general. Further, even deposit mobilization is not possible at least for the first three years, till a satisfactory credit rating is obtained.
- That leaves the option of borrowing from foreign institutions, which is difficult in the first place, due to RBI's requirement of at least two credit ratings. Further, very few foreign institutions are willing to give rupee denominated loans. Thus the MFI taking foreign currency loans are subject to exchange risks, which they cannot handle.

Lack of Commercial Orientation

Striving to make the customers credit available at low cost with subsidies and grants, most of the alternate MFIs achieve a lot of success in their programs in the initial period, but they fail to maintain the same record in the long-run because of lack of commercial orientation thus making it unsustainable.

Lack of Proper Governance and Accountability

Governance and accountability are limited in case of non-profits and need to be improved. Their boards must be made aware of their financial liabilities in case of failure. The lenders should be more stringent and insist on nominating a few directors.

Isolated and Scattered

The alternate MFIs are isolated and scattered. There is no proper coordination among them and also there is lack of information dissemination.

MOVING FORWARD

Most of the issues stated above are being tackled at various levels and the initiatives if successful, could substantially remove these hurdles. Over the last few years, the Government of India has been encouraging micro-finance as an alternative to IRDP type of poverty alleviation programs because of the sustainability of micro-finance activities. In the last two Budget Speeches, the Finance Ministers have talked about the need to enhance the reach of the MFIs. The RBI also made a special mention of micro-finance in its credit policy announced in April 1999. The RBI has established a micro-credit cell; NABARD has set up a Micro-credit Innovations Department, while HUDCO is also formulating a similar plan. The issue of inappropriate legal form for MFIs is being addressed by a Task Force setup by the Reserve Bank of India, which among other things is looking into the regulatory and legal issues concerning micro-finance in India.

An increasing number of MFIs have begun to address the issue of financial sustainability of their programs and have started taking effective steps towards achieving sustainability. Many of them have increased their interest rates, at least to cover their costs. Some of them have taken steps to convert themselves into for-profit corporations and have sought commercial investors to invest in them. These will not only make micro-finance more commercially oriented but will also increase the quality of governance.

Another welcome development in the Indian micro-finance sector in recent years has been the establishment of networks of micro-finance practitioners. These networks not only help in creating awareness but also help in formation, experience sharing etc. These could also develop into a Self Regulatory Organization of micro-finance institutions.

CONCLUSION

After the pioneering efforts of the last ten years, the micro-finance scene in India has reached a takeoff point. With some effort substantial progress can be made in taking MFIs to the next orbit of significance and sustainability. This needs innovative and forward-looking policies, based on the ground realities of successful MFIs. This, combined with a commercial approach from the MFIs in making micro-finance financially sustainable, will make this sector vibrant and help achieve its single-minded mission of providing financial services to the poor.

Regularities in Indian Stock Market: An Investigation

—*Harish Kumar**

—*Dr. Malabika Deo***

INTRODUCTION

Most of the modern finance theories are formulated based on the assumption of efficient capital market. An efficient market is understood to be a market, where the price of the security reflects the market's best estimate of their expected return on risk, taking into account all the information material to their expected return on risk, taking into account all the information material to their pricing. Hence, the securities are supposed to be fairly price at any point of time. Thus, there does not exist any overvalued securities offering higher or lower return than the expected help the investor get abnormal return, by identifying undervalued and over valued securities and formulating the strategy

* Faculty Member, Department of Commerce, Pondicherry University, Pondicherry.

** Department of Commerce, Pondicherry University, Pondicherry.

accordingly. Thus market efficiency has an influence on the investment strategy can help the investor get abnormal return, by identifying undervalued and over valued securities and formulating the strategy accordingly. Thus market efficiency has an influence trying to pick winners will be a waste of time, if otherwise excess return can be made by currently pricing winners.

The term market efficiency is used to explain the relationship between information and share prices movement in the stock market. An efficient capital market is a market that is efficient in processing information. In this market information is evaluated as it arrives and prices instantaneously adjust to a new level and the security prices equal their intrinsic value at all times. Therefore, an investor cannot consistently earn excess returns by undertaking fundamental analysis or technical analysis.

The security prices in an efficient capital market fully reflect their investment value. The market has the capability to instantaneously impound the given set of information into the pricing process. It is impossible to consistently make abnormal returns using a trading strategy based on a given set of information when the markets are efficient. This postulate is based on the premises that:

(1) all in vestors have cost-less access to currently available information about the future;

(2) they are good analysts; and

(3) they pay close attention to the market process and adjust their holding appropriately.

Till the late seventies, empirical studies supported the view that capital markets are informationally efficient. Many models related to security valuation have been based on this concept of 'informational efficiency of capital market. However, the late seventies and eighties brought in evidences questioning the validity and highlighting various anomalies related to the capital market efficiency. There are many focused studies that demonstrated the possible trading strategies yielding abnormal rates of returns using the historical data and publicly available information ruling out the efficiency of market. The empirical studies evidencing the inefficiency are broadly related to:

- the low P/E effect,
- low priced stocks
- insignificant firm effects,
- market overreaction,
- the January effect,
- holiday effect
- persistence of technical analysts, and
- the day of the week effect.

As stated earlier, in an efficient market stock returns are identical for all days of the week. However, the financial researchers have observed that the stock returns are not identical across the time periods. Most specifically, the researchers have found that the Monday return is significantly negative and Friday experiences a high positive return. This observation is generally referred to as 'day of the week effect' or 'the weekend effect.'

The most satisfactory explanation that has been given for the negative returns on Monday is that usually the most unfavourable news appears during the weekends. These unfavourable news influence the majority of the investors negatively, causing them to sell on the following Monday. Other possible reasons behind his anomaly identified by financial researchers include settlement effects, measurement error, specialist related biases and trading pattern of individual and institutional investors.

Thus if an investor has the ability to compound the price swings in earning extra normal returns, he counters the principle of market efficiency. In addition, any systematic pattern of price changes across days of the week may also suggest some trading strategy to earn abnormal returns. This study attempts to focus on stock return variability across days of the week and try to find out the existence of the day of the week effect in stock return in the Indian Stock market based on regularity or otherwise of returns across the days in a week.

PREVIOUS STUDIES

The studies on the behaviour of stock returns to find out the day of the week effect by using different methodologies have grown substantially over the years. French (1980), and Gibbons and Hess (1981) document a weekend effect with a low or negative return on Mondays in the US stock market. Smirlok and Starks (1983), Rogalski (1984) found that most of the negative returns on Friday closing price to the Monday closing price take place when the market is closed over weekends rather than during the trading day on Monday. Maurice (1988), Dyl and Holland (1990) opine that individual investor trades odd-lots more than the institutional investors and this specific event that may cause day of the week effect is NYSE, Ziemba (1993) in his study reported that Japanese market experiences significant Tuesday returns. Fishe and Laiser (1993) confirmed negative Monday return due to negative effect. Abraham and Ikenberry (1994) observed that the Monday return following negative Friday return was significantly negative nearly 80 per cent of time. Similarly, Athanassakos and Robinson (1994) also observed that 72 per cent of Monday return following negative Friday supported negative return. Sias and Starks (1995) in their study argues that the trading behavior of institutional investors is the main reason behind the Monday effect. According to Chow *et al.* (1997), it is possible to exploit the day of the week effect to generate positive returns by following the sorting strategy prescribed by them. Kamara (1997) found a significant decline in Monday seasonal due to increase in ration of institutional trading volume and evidence that small-cap returns exhibited a significant Monday seasonal throughout the study period. Wang and Erickson (1997) in their study also reported similar results. Kiymaz *et al.*(2002) in their study investigate day of the week effect on volatility of major stock market in conditional variance framework. Their study reports the presence of this anomaly in Canada, Germany, Japan, U.S. and U.K. Berument *et al.* (2004) investigates the day of the week effect on return and volatility for Istanbul Stock Exchange and reported a strong presence of the day of the week effect in the market. The phenomenon of day of the week effect was not only present in the equity market, but it is also detected in the Treasury-bill market (Flannery and Protopapadakis, 1988), in the commodity and stock futures markets (Carnal, 1985; Dyl and Maberly, 1986), and in the foreign exchange market (Corha and Rad, 1994).

In the Indian stock market, there are a few studies on the day of the week effect. Chaudhuri (1991) supported the presence of weekend effect/day of the week effect in the daily return of BSE SENSEX for the period June 1988 to January 1990 through Kruskal-Wallies test. Broca (1992) presented unequivocal evidence as to the day of the week effect but concluded that the trading strategy based on this evidence is ineffective when compared to a naïve 'buy and hold' strategy. In another study Poshakwale (1996) tested the weekend effect by using BSE national index during the period January 1987 to October 1994 by applying first order auto correlation and supported the presence of weekend effect. Arumugan (1999) in his study observed positive Friday return and significant negative Monday return in bear phase. Anshuman and Goswami (1999) in their study reported that Friday show were above average positive return and Tuesdays shows below average negative returns. Their study rejected the settlement error, size-effect, and settlement effect and badla mechanism as possible factors behind the phenomenon of weekend effect. Amanualla and Thiripalraju (2001) tested whether the carry-forward transactions in different periods have any impact on weekend effect. The results form the sample period strongly supported the weekend effect during the period of ban on badla transactions. The study also shows a reversal in weekend effect, i.e., positive Monday return and negative Friday return in modified carry forward transaction and revised modified carry forward transactions. Further, the study reported that there is a consistent positive return on Wednesday and consistent negative return on Tuesday due to the possible impact of NSE on weekend effect. Sarma (2004) also confirmed the existence of day of the week effect in the Indian stocks markets. Nath and Dalvi (2004) reported that before introduction of rolling settlement in January 2002, Monday and Friday were significant days. But after the introduction of rolling settlement, Friday becomes significant. The study asserts that Indian capital market is not efficient and the market is yet to price the rise appropriately. Bhattacharya *et al.* (2005) examines the stability of the day of the week effect in returns and volatility at the Indian security market. They tried to explain this anomaly with respect to reporting and non-reporting week of the banks. Gupta (2006) in his study examined day of the week effect in Indian stock market after the introduction of compulsory rolling settlement system and confirmed the presents of this anomaly during the study period.

Though various studies have largely accounted for all possible factors responsible for the day of the week effect, they differed widely in their findings. Hence, it is difficult to give any specific factor(s) responsible for his anomaly. Thus, this day of the week effect, in sharp contrast to the theories of efficient market, was considered as a puzzle and despite different theories and explanations, so far the puzzle has not been satisfactorily resolved. As more and more empirical evidences are obtained from different stock market all over the world, the puzzle seems to have increased.

Further, most of these studies have been based on data of mid-1980s and mid-1990s and have taken the closing values of the respective indices in return compilation process with the implied assumption that trading is done at the closing price. However, there would not be any need to make such an assumption in case an average of high, low, opening and closing values are taken (Sarma). Thus, it would be pertinent to retest the conclusions drawn by earlier studies in view of the changes in the wider economic scenario in India, widened choice of benchmark portfolios, and methods of measurement techniques. With this background, the present study examines the presence of day of the week effect in stock returns in India.

DATA AND PERIOD OF THE STUDY

The PROWESS database provides information regarding the daily opening, high, low and close values of the SENSEX, and Nifty indices. The study used this data related to the period spanning from January 1st 1997 to June 30th 2005 comprising a total of 2139 observations for each of the indices.

Ideally, individual stock price should be used for such an analysis, since the index data suffers from inherent limitations in the face of non-synchronous trading and omission of dividends. These may lead to statistical problems such as under-statement of returns. Autocorrelation and distortions in estimated variances. However, French *et al.*, (1987) have shown that the results are broadly similar when the daily values of the S and P 500 index as well as 30 actively traded shares on the NYSE are taken.

METHODOLOGY

The earlier studies had used the closing values for return generating procedure with an implied assumption of trading done at the closing values there would not be any need for such a restrictive trading assumption in case an average of the available opening, high, low and closing values is used. The continuously compounded annual rate of returns is a well-accepted approach to measuring the daily returns. The natural log of daily relative mean index value is, thus, the measure of daily return used in this study. The formula is stated below:

$$Rt = \text{In}\left(\frac{I_t}{I_{t-1}}\right)$$

where,

Rt = return on day 't'

I_t = Index mean value on day 't'

I_{t-1} = index mean value on day 't-1'

In = natural log

The returns so generated are classified day-wise, from Monday to Friday and their equalities and volatilities are measured.

For testing whether mean returns are constant across all five days of the week or whether they exhibit statistically significant differences, a non-parametric test method has been employed. This is because of their robustness arising from lack of restrictive assumption such as population normality and homoscedastic variances. Thus, the usual one-way analysis of variance is replaced by its non-parametric alternative, the Kruskal-Wallis (K-W) test.

K-W test is non-parametric tests for testing the null hypothesis that K independent random sample comes from identical populations against the alternative hypothesis that the means of these samples are not all equal.

The K-W test requires the entire set of observations to be ranked-higher the value, higher the rank and vice versa then arranges into n I*5 matrix where ni represents the rank of the return and columns represents the day of the week Monday through Friday. The formula for calculating the test statistic 'H' is as follows:

$$H = \left[\frac{12}{N(N+1)} \sum_{j=1}^{5} \frac{R_J^2}{n_j} \right] - 3(N+1)$$

where:

R_j = sum of the ranks in the jth column

N_j = number of case sin the jth column

N = sum of observation in all the column

Since the sampling distribution of 'H' is asymptotically leptokurtic based on four degrees of freedom, the critical value is 13.28 at one per cent level of significance for the given four degrees of freedom. If the computed value of 'H' is greater than the critical value, the null hypothesis cannot be accepted. Conversely, if the computed value of 'H' is less than the critical value, the alternative hypothesis cannot be accepted.

HYPOTHESIS

For each week day mean daily returns and return volatility have been calculated over the entire period of study and then compared. Accordingly, the hypotheses to be tested are:

H0: There are no differences in the average return on stock indices across the days of the week.

H1: There are differences in the average return on stick indices across the days of the week.

ANALYSIS AND DISCUSSION

Testing for Statistical significance: Equality of Returns

Tables 5.1, 5.2 and 5.3 present the descriptive statistics of the day of the week returns for the three selected indices along with that of the comprehensive sample - 'all days' - in addition to the computed 'H' statistics. It is clear from the Tables 5.1, 5.2 and 5.3 that the daily means returns are zero or almost zero for all the portfolios - SENSEX, and Nifty, during the study period. The distribution of daily returns tends to be leptokurtic with long tails and many centric observations. All the indices given negative returns on Fridays and all the values of the days descriptive statistics are very closely coinciding sending strong evidence as to the 'weekend effect. The standard deviation of the portfolio increased with the degree of diversification. This is neither surprising nor contrary the expectations. The portfolio construction is neither random nor based on Markowitz selectivity criterion. Standard deviation of all the indices returns is highest

Table 5.1: BSE SENSEX Day-wise Summary Statistics on Dated Returns

	Monday	Tuesday	Wednesday	Thursday	Friday	All Days
Mean	0.0002	-0.0005	0.0011	0.0003	-0.0007	0.00008
Median	0.0009	0.0000	0.0008	0.0005	-0.0002	0.00048
Standard Deviation	0.0909	0.00917	0.00778	0.00566	0.00609	0.02392
Skewness	-3.310	-2.192	5.897	-0.325	-0.227	-0.0314
Kurtosis	26.166	74.584	78.330	2.988	1.997	36.813
Range	0.12	0.20	0.13	0.05	0.005	0.11
Number of Observations	429	428	429	428	425	2139
'H' value					27.8407	

Table 5.2: S and P CNX Nifty Day-wise Summary Statistics on Daily Returns

	Monday	Tuesday	Wednesday	Thursday	Friday	All Days
Mean	0.0011	0.0007	0.0032	0.0012	-0.0001	0.0012
Median	-0.0001	-0.0001	0.0012	0.0008	-0.0004	0.0004
Standard Deviation	0.03093	0.00534	0.03596	0.03636	0.00557	0.02283
Skewness	19.238	-0.611	20.089	-20.089	-0.279	3.656
Kurtosis	388.796	2.348	409.632	411.513	1.188	242.695
Range	0.68	0.05	0.76	0.76	0.04	0.428
Number of Observations	429	428	429	428	425	21.39
'H' value					17.3631	

Table 5.3: Actual and Expected Multiple Comparison Values

	$\lvert R_{\mu} - R_{\mu} \rvert$		$Z\left(a/K(K-1)\right)^{\left(N(N+1)/12\right)^{1/2}} \left[\frac{1}{n_{\mu}} + \frac{1}{n_{\mu}}\right]^{1/2}$			
	SENSEX	NIFTY	Z	$\left(a/K(K-1)\right)$	$\left(N^{(N+1/12)}\right)^{1/2}$	$\left[\frac{1}{n_{\mu}} + \frac{1}{n_{\mu}}\right]^{1/2}$
Monday-Tuesday	113.664	98.263	2.575	507.662	0.08892	96.817
Monday-Wednesday	7.267	4.336	2.575	507.662	0.08892	96.389
Monday-Thursday	19.773	32.221	2.575	507.662	0.00892	96.719
Monday-Friday	120.831	137.669	2.575	507.662	0.08815	97.293
Tuesday-Wednesday	109.296	108.26	2.575	507.662	0.08832	97.289
Tuesday-Thursday	98.263	86.261	2.575	507.662	0.08871	96.271
Tuesday-Friday	8.412	20.226	2.575	507.662	0.08819	97.289
Wednesday-Thursday	19.263	16.226	2.575	507.662	0.08839	96.279
Wednesday-Friday	123.229	101.226	2.575	507.662	0.08879	97.881
Thursday-Friday	102.669	61.226	2.575	507.662	0.00891	96.718

for Mondays. Further, it also reveals that Mondays' standard deviation of SENSEX and Nifty are more than their respective average of 'all days' standard deviation during the study period. For all the indices, Wednesday register the highest positive return. For SENSEX, Thursday and Friday register negative returns while for Nifty Friday shows negative returns. However, for SENSEX and Nifty Friday shows the lowest return. All the indices appear to be most attractive on Mondays from the view point of mean returns and standard deviations. Considering the Kurtosis and the range figures SENSEX relatively shows some semblance of normality. Wide variations are observed across the week-days within and among the indices.

To test whether the differences in the mean returns across the weekdays are statistically significant. 'H' statistic is computed. The critical value of 'H' is abnormally higher than the critical value of all indices. Thus, the null hypothesis is rejected. This provides evidence as to the presence of regularity in common stock returns in India during the study period.

PATTERN OF DEVIATION

By employing multiple comparison procedure it is possible to find out which pair shows significant deviation from one another and uncover the general patter of high low tendencies in the data. For a given overall level of significance level of μ decide # Xμ, if

$$\left|R_{\mu} - R_{\mu}\right| \geq Z\left({}^{a}\!/\!_{K(K-1)}\right)^{\left({}^{N(N+1)}\!/\!_{12}\right)^{1/2}} \left[\frac{1}{n_{\mu}} + \frac{1}{n_{\mu}}\right]^{1/2}$$

where:

μ	= 1,2 . . . K-1
v	= u + 1 . . . K
K	= 5
N	= total number of daily returns
n	= number of daily means in the uth and v[th] column
R	= average rank sum of the uth and i[th] column
$z\left(\frac{a}{K(K-1)}\right)$	= the upper percentage point of the unit normal distribution for a given significant level

Whose value for 99 per cent confidence level is 2.575. The required calculations are presented in Table 5.4 and 5.5.

Table 5.4: Deviation of Actual From Expected (Average Risk Difference)

	SENSEX	NIFTY
Monday-Friday	16.847	1.446
Monday-Wednesday	-89.122	-92.052
Monday-Thursday	-77.006	-64.498
Monday-Friday	23.538	40.376
Tuesday-Wednesday	12.007	10.971
Tuesday-Thursday	1.992	-10.01
Tuesday-Friday	-88.877	-77.063
Wednesday-Thursday	-77.016	-80.053
Wednesday-Friday	16.382	-25.348
Thursday-Friday	5.951	-35.492

Table 5.5: Trading Strategy (Annual Returns Generated)

	SENSEX	NIFTY
Monday-Thursday	2.93	31.77
Monday-Friday	20.63	29.92
Wednesday-Friday	7.91	35.27
Buy and hold	17.26	27.82

Table 5.5 shows that Monday-Tuesday, Monday-Friday and Wednesday-Friday sets have positive deviation for all the indices. However, Monday-Friday sets for all the indices have the highest positive deviation. Tuesday-Wednesday-sets also have positive deviations, although very low, for all the indices. Thus, in general, Indian stock markets exhibit regularities in the equity return and have scope for questioning its market efficiency.

IMPLICATION FOR MARKET EFFICIENCY

Through pair-wise multiple comparison procedure, it is observed that Monday-Tuesday, Monday-Friday, and Wednesday-Friday have positive deviation for all the indices. These observations must consequently lead us to designing a trading strategy exploiting the possibility of making abnormal returns. A comparison of annual rates of return generated by a passive strategy of 'by and hold' and various active strategies of 'buying Monday and selling Thursday' or 'buying Monday and selling Friday' or buying Wednesday and selling Friday' is presented in Table 5.6. For all the indices mean returns of the active strategies turned out to be lower than the 'buy and hold' strategy for the field. With transaction cost this would further reduce, even whip out, any profit the investor could have earned through the active strategy mentioned above. The active strategy is of little use may be because the study period is characteristic of a highly unsettled economic environment and the fact that the indices underwent frequent shuffling and reshuffling unconnected to the principles of diversification. Broca (1992) also found the return resulting from pursuing a trading strategy based on the observed regularity of return being less than a naïve 'by and hold strategy' in spite of his strong evidence as to the Wednesday having the lowest returns and Friday the highest. However this does not mean that knowledge of persistent stock market behaviour pattern on week days has not value whatsoever. An individual can increase the expected return to his investment by altering the timing of routinely scheduled transactions.

CONCLUSION

The assumption of efficient Capital Market is the base of the modern finance theories. However, whether markets are efficient or not is a matter to be investigated before applying the postulate to finance theories. Many researches have challenged the application of dictums of finance theories on the ground of non-existent efficient capital market. The researchers have discovered many anomalies in various capital market theories, doubting the existence of an efficient market. One of the widely reported market anomaly is Day of the Week Effect. This anomaly suggest that adoption of trading strategy will enable the investor to make abnormal return if market is not efficient. In this study an attempt is made to investigate the presence of the day of the week effect or otherwise in Indian stock market. The study is conducted on the log return data of Sensex and Nifty since 1st January, 1997 to 30th June, 2004. The data source is Prowess data base. A total of 2139 observations of Sensex and Nifty have been taken as the base of the present investigation. The data has been analyzed with the help of a non-parametric tool i.e. Kruskal-Wallis Test. The analysis provides evidence as to the presence of day of the week effect in stock returns. It confirms the evidence of earlier studies as to the leptokurtic distribution of equity returns across the indices. An examination of daily returns of these indices during this period shows evidence of significant variation according to the day of the week. This contradicts to the random walk hypothesis as a descriptive model for common stock price movements in India. Wednesday show consistently highest returns and Friday show consistently negative returns for all the indices. Through a pair wise comparison procedure, it is found that Monday-Tuesday, Monday-Friday and Wednesday-Friday have highest positive deviations for all the indices. But a simple trading strategy designed to exploit this empirical regularities could not out-perform a naïve 'by and hold' policy over the study period. A benefit, however, accruing to investors form knowledge of the variation is that by altering the timing of routinely scheduled transactions they could increase the expected returns on investments.

REFERENCES

Abraham, Abraham and Ikenberry L. David 1994. "The Individual Investor and the Weekend Effect", *Journal of Financial and Quantitative Analysis*. 29: 2.263-277.

Amanulla, S. and Thiripalraju, M. 2001, "Week-end Effect: New Evidence from the Indian Stock Market", *Vikalpa.* 26: 2: 33-50.

Anshuman, R. and Goswami, R. 1992, "Day of the Week Effect on Bombay Stock Exchange". A paper Presented at the Third Capital Market Conference, Indian Institute of Capital Market, Mumbai.

Arumugan, 1998, "Dy of the Week Effect in Stock Returns: An Empirical Evidence from the Indian Stock Market". *Prajan,* 27(2): 171-191.

Berument, Hakan and Kiymaz Halit, 2001, "The Day of the Week and Stock Market Volatality". *Journal of Economics and Finance,* 25(2): 181-192.

Berument, Hakan, Kiyamaz, Halil, 2004, "The Day of the Week Effect and Stock Market Volatality: Evidence From Developed Market", *Journal of Economics and Finance* 7(2): 60-67.

Bhattacharya, K. Sarkar, and Nand Mukhopadhyay, 2003, "Stability of the Day of the Week Effect in Return and in Volatility at the Indian Capital Market: A GARCH Approach with Proper Mean Specification". *Applied Financial Economics,* 13(5): 553-563.

Broca, Dilbagh, 1992, "Day of the Week Patterns in the Indian Stock Market", *Decision,* 19(2): 57-64.

Canbell, J.Y and Y Hanao, 1992, "Predictable Stock Returns in the United States and Japan: A study of Long-term Capital Market Integration., "Journal of Finance, 43:69.

Carnal, B., 1985, "The weekly Patterns in Stock Returns Cash Verses Futters: A Note," Journal of Finance 40, 583-588.

Chan, K.C., A. Karolyi and R.M. Stulz 1991, "Global Financial Market and the Risk Performance on U.S Equity". *Journal of Financial Economics,* 32: 137-167.

Chaudhury, S.K. 1991, "Seasonality in Share Returns" Preliminary Evidence on Day of the Week Effect". *Chartered Accountant* 40(8): 107-9.

Choudhury, T. 2000, "Day of the Week Effect in Emerging Asian Stock Markets: Evidence from GARCH Model." *Applied Financial Economics,* 20(3): 235-742.

Corha, F. and A.T. Rad 1994, "Statistical Proprieties of Daily Returns. Evidence from European Stock Market." *Journal of Business Finance and Accounting,* 20: 271-282.

Damodaran, Aswath, 1989, "The Weekend Effect in Information Releases: A Study of Earnings and Dividend Announcements". *The Review of Financial Studies*, 2(4): 607-623.

Dyl, E. and Maberly, E., 1986, "The Weekly Pattern in Stock Index Futures: A Further Note". *Journal of Finance*, 41(5): 1149-1152.

Dyl and Holland, C.W., 1987, "Why a Weekend Effect: A Comment". *Journals of Portfolio Management*, 16(2): 199-228.

Fama, Eugene, F., 1965, "The Behavioural of Stock Market Price". *Journal of Finance*, 15(5): 34-105.

Flannery, M. and Protopapadakis, A., 1988, "From T-bills to Comm Market". *Journal of Future Markets*, 7: 169-181.

French, K.R., 1980, "Stock Returns and the Weekend Effect". *Journal of Financial Economics*, 8(1): 55-69.

French, K.R.G., W. Schwent and R.F. Stambaugh, 1987, "Expected Stock Returns and Volatility". *Journal of Financial Economics*, 19: 3-27.

Geo, Lie and Kling, Gerhard, 2005, "Calendar Effects in Chinese Stock Market", *Journal of Economics and Finance*, 5: 75-88.

Gibbons, Michael. R. and Hess, Patrick, 1981, "Day of the Week Effect and Asset Returns", *Journal of Business*, 54(4): 579-596.

Gupta, 2003, "Day of the week Effect on the Indian Stock Market: New Evidence." *The ICFAI Journal of Applied Finance*, 12(8): 5-14.

Hsieh, D.A., 1988, "The Statistical Properties of Daily Foreign Exchange Rate 1974-1983", *Journal of International Economics*, 24: 129-145.

Levi, Maurice, 1988, "Weekend Effects in Stock Market Returns: An Overview". In: Elroy Dimson (ed.), *Stock Market Anomalies*. Cambridge: Cambridge University Press.

Nath, C. Golka, and Daliv, Monoj, 2004, "Day of the Week Effect and Market Efficiency: Evidence from Indian Equality Market Using High Frequency Data of National Stock Exchange". *ICFAI Journal of Applied Finance*, 7(5): 445-456.

Panman, S.H., 1987, "The Distribution of Earning News Over Time and Seasonalities in Aggregate Stock Returns". *Journal of Financial Economics*, 18: 199-228.

Poshakwala, Sunil, 1996, "Evidence on Weak from Efficiency and Day of the Week Returns on Trading and Non-Trading Periods: A Note, "Journal of Finance 34, 6: 603-616.

Rogalski J. Richard, 1984, "New Findings Regarding Day of the Week Returns on Trading and Non-Trading Periods: A Note", *Journal of Finance*, 6: 1603-1615.

Sarma, S.N., 2004, "Stock Market Seasonality in an Emerging Market". *Vikalpa*, 29(3): 35-42.

Smirlock, Michael and Leura Starks, 1986, "Day of the Week and Intraday Effects in Stock Returns". *Journal of Financial Economics*, 17: 197-210.

Wang, K. Li, Y. and Erickson, J. 1997. "A New Look at the Monday Effect". *Journal of Finance*, 52: 2171-2187.

Institutional Credit and Agricultural Development in Orissa

—*Bibhudatta Nayak*

Financial involvement, either own or borrowed from formal and/or informal sources, is indispensable for taking up an economic activity, be it land based or non-land based. In Orissa where agriculture predominates, large-scale rural population and absolute poverty prevails, significance of credit for economic development assumes greater importance. Institutional credit has a major role to play for the development of both farm as well as non-farm sectors.

INSTITUTIONAL CREDIT SCENARIO

Before entering the institutional credit scenario it would be appropriate to have a *rendezvous* on the development of institutional finance in India as well as

* Assistant General Manager (Economic Services), National Bank for Agriculture and Rural Development, Orissa Regional Office, Bhubaneswar. Views expressed in the paper are of the author only, not of the institution he belongs to.

in Orissa. Advent of banking in Hindustan dates back to the Eighteenth Century when the Bank of Hindustan was established in 1770. By the end of Nineteenth Century there were five banks out of which two were registered as scheduled banks later on. In 1951 there were as many as 566 banks including 474 non-scheduled banks in India. The turning point in banking sector was the nationalization of banks in 1969 that widened the scope for institutional lending in the agriculture sector. During the three and half decades period after nationalization of banks the banking policies, programmes and operations in India have endeavored to achieve the broader objectives of nationalization by reorienting the banking system towards a larger social purpose. Consequently the banking sector has undergone structural transformation in both qualitative and quantitative terms and made considerable headway with realization of national goals and priorities.

Now three mainstream credit institutions; Cooperative Banks which were initiated during the onset of 20th century, the Commercial Banks which were involved in rural banking from late sixties and the Regional Rural Banks created in 1975, establish the foundation of rural credit supply network in India. Expansion of branch network has brought down the average population covered per branch in India to 13,000 in 2003 from 88,000 in 1961. The population per branch in Orissa was further low at 12,309 (SFP 2005).

Advent of Banking in Orissa dates back to 1909 when the first bank named Puri Joint Stock Bank was set up in Orissa. The next were Cuttack Joint Stock

Bank and Jagannath Bank in 1919. Of these only Cuttack Joint Stock Bank stood the test of time up to 1954 when it merged with the United Bank of India Ltd. The Imperial Bank of India made its debut in Orissa with the opening of a branch at Berhampur (Ganjam) in 1921 followed by another at Cuttack in the same year. In the erstwhile princely state of Mayurbhanj the banking message was aptly conveyed by Mayurbhanj State Bank, which was started in 1938 at Baripada and expanded in the state by opening of branches at Karanjia and Rairangpur. After twenty-two years of independent existence the bank merged with State Bank of India in 1961. By 1949 end the state had only 7 scheduled Commercial Banks having network of 14 branches. By that time our country had as many as 92 banks with 2788 branches. The total deposits held by the banks in Orissa was just Rs. 2 crore against all India deposit of Rs. 842 crore.

Banks then hardly answered the financial needs of common man, who usually fell into the vice like clutches of greedy village money-lenders. Banks were blissfully providing credit to big traders, merchants and established dealers. Institutional credit flow for agriculture sector during the initial Five Year Plans was very meager, around 2-3 per cent of total bank credit. During the Annual plans it was abysmally low, at 0.4 per cent in 1968. It slightly improved after the nationalization of banks, up to 10.4% in 1980 and 14.8% in 1991.

Ground Level Credit Flow

Ground Level Credit (GLC) flows in various sectors. As such they can be categorized into Agriculture –

short-term (Crop Loan) and long- and medium-term (ATL). Non Farm Sector (NFS) and Other Priority Sector (OPS) including Govt. sponsored schemes. Commensurate with the augmented need, the GLC flow in Orissa increased about fourteen times during last ten years (Table 6.1). As it can be seen from Table 1, the annual GLC flow has recorded increase over the previous years in all the years except 2002-03. The Crop Loan disbursements remained more or less steady as compared to Agricultural Term Lending (ATL). Agricultural term loans, which contribute towards capital formation in agriculture recorded negative annual growth in three out of ten years during 1993-94 and 2003-04.

Trend of ground level credit flow in Orissa, especially after 1999-2000, was more influenced by the changes in the lending for non-agricultural areas. Advances for housing, vehicles and personal loans contributed more for the bulky growth in non-agriculture sectors. In absolute sense, in the agriculture front while crop loan increased almost ten times during past ten years growth in ATL remained relatively slow, it increased just less than three times during the past ten years. But in relative sense share of ATL in GLC ripped down continuously from 25% in 1993-94 to 5% ion 2003-04. Share of Crop Loan in GLC was receding after 1998-99.

An analysis of further break ups of the ground level credit flow for the past six years (during 1998-99 and 2003-04) reveals that ATL to sectors like plantation and horticulture (P and H), farm mechanization (FM), storage and market yard (SMY) and animal husbandry, especially poultry and sheep/goat/pigs, recorded

Table 6.1: Year-wise and Sector-wise Flow of GLC in Orissa

(Rs. Crore)

Year	Total GLC	A I (%)	Crop Loan	A I (%)	% of GLC	ATL	A I (%)	% of GLC	NFS and OPS	% of GLC	A I (%)
1993-94	335	-	120	-	36	84	-	25	131	39	-
1994-95	499	49	163	36	33	107	27	21	229	46	75
1995-96	686	38	252	54	37	126	17	18	309	45	35
1996-97	919	34	276	10	30	165	31	18	478	52	55
1997-98	1069	16	326	18	30	142	(-)14	14	601	56	26
1998-99	1077	1	455	40	42	150	5	14	472	44	(-)21
1999-00	1261	17	522	15	41	149	(-)0.3	12	589	47	25
2000-01	1842	46	623	19	34	200	34	11	1018	55	73
2001-02	2496	36	754	21	30	175	(-)13	7	1567	63	54
2002-03	2433	(-)2	870	15	36	177	1	7	1386	57	(-)12
2003-04	4551	87	1107	27	24	220	24	5	3224	71	132

Source: SFP 1999, 2002 and 2005.

marginal increase (Table 6.2). The increase was mainly due to crop diversification, commercialization in agriculture and taking up of support activities under agriculture and allied sectors. The increase in credit flow under FM may be due to spread of mechanization particularly in tillage and harvesting of paddy, the major crop in Orissa agriculture, and to some extent opportunities for custom hire. Plummeting availability of draught animals and expansion of rural road network augmented the need for Farm mechanization Revision of norms for financing tractors and other machineries also contributed for rise in credit advancements in FM. An important sector in agriculture, irrigation, however recorded reduced credit flow for four years after 1998-99. One of the reasons for the poor credit absorption in Minor Irrigation may be due to construction of major and medium irrigation projects under RIDF assistance as well as introduction of subsidy linked minor irrigation schemes like PLI and OFWM Schemes. Credit deployment in Land Development has also shown steadiness in the past a few years.

During 2003-04, 29 per cent of GLC flow in Orissa was for Agriculture, of which 83% was for Seasonal Agricultural Operations (SAO) or crop loans. NFS accounted for only 6 per cent of the GLC flow whereas other priority sector had the lion's share with almost two thirds (65%) of the total ground level credit disbursements. The mammoth size of loans under OPS was due to increasing credit flow under consumer articles, computers, vehicles, housing, education and personal loan.

Table 6.2: GLC in Orissa – Sector-wise Distribution

(Rs. Crore)

Sl.	Particulars	1998-99	1999-00	2000-01	2001-02	2002-03	2003-04
I.	Crop Loans	455	523	633	754	870	1107
II.	Term Loans	150	149	182	175	177	220
a	Minor Irrigation	26	17	30	21	22	26
b	Land Development	12	6	11	11	12	13
c	Farm Mechanization	34	38	48	50	56	51
d	Plantation and Horticulture	8	11	14	13	10	37
e	Dairy Development	10	10	17	16	12	11
f	Poultry	4	5	8	9	9	9
g	Sheep/Goat/Piggery	10	12	13	15	12	17
h	Fisheries	8	7	9	9	14	12
i	Forestry/Wasteland Devt.	1	2	3	4	3	3
j	Storage and Market Yard	2	5	7	8	8	9
k	Others	35	37	23	19	18	31
Total Agricultural Credit		**605**	**672**	**816**	**929**	**1047**	**1327**
III.	**Non Farm Sector**	**135**	**199**	**187**	**255**	**146**	**272**
IV.	**Other Priority Sector**	**336**	**390**	**869**	**1313**	**1241**	**2952**
Ground Level Credit Flow		**1077**	**1261**	**1872**	**2496**	**2433**	**4551**

Source: SFP 2002 and 2005

SUPPLY SYNDROME OF INSTITUTIONAL CREDIT

NABARD prepared Potential Linked Credit Plan (PLPs) for each and every district which present financially and technically vetted realistic estimations of credit requirements. As per PLP projections targets (potential) for credit flow under four broad sectors viz., Agriculture, Non-Farm Sector and Other Priority Sector and disbursement of GLC for years from 1998-99 to 2003-04 were presented in Table 6.3. While the achievements were around 80-95 per cent under agriculture it was fluctuating between 52 and 96 per cent of the targets under non-farm sector.

Within Agriculture sector Term Loan disbursement failed to match with the targeted credit flow. Even though there was potential for term loan in agriculture and willingness on the part of lending institutions (target was much more than the achievement), credit outflow for ATL remained low. The broad reason was lack of effective demand from the borrowers (Nayak, 2005).

Adequacy of Farm Credit

If we estimate the average crop loan in Orissa by taking into the net sown area and crop loan disbursement in the corresponding years then, as can be observed from Table 6.4, the average crop loan off take was Rs. 1,926 per hectare during 2003-04. Though it remained relatively low it was increasing over time. In absolute terms it had gone up by more than two and a half times during past five years i.e. from Rs. 753 in 1998-99 to Rs. 1,926 in 2003-04.

Table 6.3: Targets and Achievements of Institutional Credit Flow in Orissa

(Rs. Crore)

Particulars	1998-99	1999-00	2000-01	2001-02	2002-03	2003-04
I. Crop Loans						
Targets	393	525	663	750	904	974
Achievements	455	523	633	754	870	1107
% Achieved	116	100	96	100	96	114
II. Term Loans						
Targets	266	283	182	379	409	420
Achievements	150	149	182	175	177	220
% Achieved	56	53	55	46	43	52
Total Agricultural Credit (I + II)						
Targets	660	808	996	1129	1313	1394
Achievements	605	672	816	929	1047	1327
% Achieved	92	83	82	82	80	95
III. Non Farm Sector						
Targets	177	240	259	266	282	290
Achievements	135	199	187	255	146	272
% Achieved	77	83	72	96	52	94
IV. Other Priority Sector						
Targets	437	443	550	697	893	1042
Achievements	336	390	869	1313	1241	2952
% Achieved	77	88	158	188	139	283
Ground Level Credit Flow						
Targets	1247	1491	1805	2093	2489	2726
Achievements	1077	1261	1872	2496	2433	4551
% Achieved	86	85	104	119	98	167

Source: SFP 2002 and 2005.

Table 6.4: Per Hectare Average Institutional Crop Loan

Year	NSA ('000 ha)	Crop loan (Rs. Crore)	Per ha. Crop loan (Rs.)
1998-1999	6048	455	753
1999-2000	6075	522	860
2000-2001	5829	623	1,025
2001-2002	5845	754	1,290
2002-2003	5680	870	1,531
2003-2004	5750*	1107	1,926

*Quick estimates.

Term loan on the other hand is lent for a longer period (Table 6.5) depending on the nature of activities. If we consider on an average of 5 years tenure of the agricultural term loan, then the average agricultural term loan would be around Rs. 1,564 per hectare. In actual practice, the per hectare institutional credit may be much higher than these estimated figures, because neither all the farm households avail institutional credit nor the institutional credit availed is utilized for the entire landholding of borrowing members.

Kissan Credit Cards

Since the announcement in the Union budget for 1998-99 for issuance of Kissan Credit Cards (KCC) Financing Institutions took all initiatives to make the scheme reach at all the eligible farmers. In a span of five years 436 lakh KCC were issued in India with a sanction of 1,11,459 crores (GoI, 2005).

In Orissa out of about 50 lakh operational holding over 25 lakh have been issued KCCs. By the end of September 2004 over 24 lakh farmers have been lent

Table 6.5: Repayment Period of Various Farm Sector Investments

Sl. No.	Investment	Specifications	Loan period	Average Unit Costs (Rs.)
I.	Minor Irrigation			
		Dugwell	11-15 years	23500-38300
		STW	9 years and above	24000-32500
		Borewell	11-15 years	45100-89400
II.	Animal Husbandry			
		Bullock local variety, Bullock cart	4 years	7500-22000
		All others	5-7 years	14400-250000
III.	Plantation and Horticulture			
		Fruit crops (acre)	9-14 years	12000-22000
		Betel vine	5-7 years	14000-90000
		Vegetable (acre)	3-7 years	36000-60000
		Floriculture (acre)	3-5 years	20000-70000
IV.	Land Development			
		Leveling	5-7 years	10000-30000
		Bench terracing	8-12 years	27000-37000
V.	Fisheries	(acre)	5-7 years	48000-250000
VI.	Forestry	(hectare)	4-10 years	12000-41000

Source: NABARD 2004.

with a cumulative of Rs. 1,559 crore of credit (GoO 2005). The cooperative sector has taken the lead by covering 84% of cardholders and lending 66% of credit. KCC scheme has been revised in October 2004 so as to cover term loans for agriculture and allied activities as well (RBI, 2004).

Micro-finance

Looking into the need for institutional credit support for consumption as well as income generating activities of the teeming millions NABARD introduced the Self Help Group approach and micro finance in 1992-93. On the strength of the ability of the SHG to manage funds financing institutes extend credit to SHG, which enables the members for taking up economic activities as also to meet their consumption needs including medical and social expenses. Apart from this, SHG movement opened up the process of social re-engineering among the women and weaker sections especially in the rural areas. By the end of March 2005, about 1,23,256 SHGs were supported with Rs. 251 crore in Orissa. This benefited approximate 127 lakh families covering most of the BPL families. The economically weaker sections through micro-finance. A major part of the bank credit lent to SHGs goes to agriculture and allied activities (Nayak, 2004).

Crop Insurance

As a safety net to crop failure due to natural calamities a Cooprehensive Crop Insurance Scheme (CCIS) was introduced in Orissa in 1985. The Scheme covered all farmers availing crop loan from a bank National Agricultural Insurance Scheme (NAIS), a more liberal and modified scheme has been introduced since 1999-2000. Under NAIS an amount of Rs. 244 crore was paid to 8.39 lakh farmers for the loss of crop over an area of 13.78 lakh hectare in Orissa (GoO, 2005).

RURAL INFRASTRUCTURE DEVELOPMENT FUND

The Government of India declared in the Annual Budget for 1995-96 about setting up of a Rural Infrastructure Development Fund (RIDF) within the NABARD for providing financial support for completion of the on-going and incomplete rural infrastructure projects. The Fund was made up of contributions from all Scheduled Commercial Banks, excluding Foreign Banks, operating in India, to the extent of shortfall in agricultural lending in the priority sector target, subject to a maximum of 1.5% of their net bank credit. The total corpus of the Fund till the RIDF X was Rs. 43,500 crore. RIDF is being utilized for providing loan assistance to the State Government in order to complete the stalled infrastructure projects and also for taking up new infrastructure projects. In Orissa Rs. 1875 crore have been sanctioned for 48,429 projects under irrigation and rural roads and bridges.

Doubling of Credit

Government of India directed in August 2004 for doubling of agricultural credit in next three years. To meet the requirement banks have taken initiatives to augment the credit flow to agriculture sector by at least 30% in 2004-05. the strategy to comply with the target is to bring in new borrowers under the coverage o credit, issuance of KCC to all eligible farmers, augmenting agricultural term lending through support of project formulation and capacity building of bank staff, encouraging progressive farmers to take up economically viable agricultural and allied activities, promoting Agri-Clinics and Agri-Business Centers, revision in Scale of Finance, motivating each rural bank branch to finance 2-3 Agricultural Projects and extend credit at least to one hundred new borrowers, etc.

As far as supply of institutional credit is concerned the formal sector always tries to tap the eligible and creditworthy borrowers. The branch network and bank staff in this state has access to almost every corner. Banks are in continuous process for revising the guidelines for smoothening the credit flow, upgrading the technology of quick operation, improving skill of the staff through training and refresher workshops, popularizing various schemes/programmes of banks, introducing new programmes, etc. The effective demand from the borrowers, however, has to be increased for a higher institutional credit flow to rural areas in general and agriculture sector in particular.

DEMAND SYNDROMES OF INSTITUTIONAL CREDIT IN ORISSA

Institutional credits flow in response to effective demand from eligible borrowers. Eligibility of a borrower refers to compliance by the borrowers to certain conditions and guidelines as put forth by the financing institutions. This system sometimes puts the illiterate rural borrower in hesitation to approach a bank for credit. Factors responsible for the low effective demand for institutional credit are discussed below:

Effective Demand

The Marginal and Small Farmers together constitute 96 per cent of total land holdings in Orissa (Table 6.6). Food security is their prime concern. Small and Marginal Farmers usually do not attempt crop diversification and large-scale capital investments in their farms due to limitations in scale. This can be a major reason for low effective demand for ATL. Rice being the staple food paddy cultivation dominates the cropping pattern in the State (77.7% of NSA). Farming practices are traditional and seldom involve heavy investments for which farmers need mostly small amount of credit and for short-term. This credit demand is met through seasonal agricultural credit.

In an exercise, it was estimated that crop loans from all banks was around 14% of total costs of cultivation of all seasonal crops in Orissa in 1999-2000 and it increases to 22% in 2003-04 (Table 6.7). We may say it remained low. But farmers usually require credit mostly to meet the expenses for farm inputs like seeds, fertilizers, pesticides, fencing, etc. Labour charges remain the largest component in the scale of finance of seasonal crops. Farmers in most cases manage to defer the wage payments up to the harvest. Application of farm inputs has remained relatively low in Orissa. Thus the demand for crop loan is also low in Orissa.

Medium and large landholdings are mostly with absentee-landlords. There is seldom a demand for huge investments in such landholdings as neither the

Table 6.6: Operational Holding in Orissa

(as per 1995-96 Agricultural Census)

Landholding category	Operational holding				
	Size	No. in '000	Percentage	Area in '000 ha.	Percentage
Marginal	Below 1 ha	2,145	54	1,064	21
Small	1-2 ha	1,106	28	1,522	29
Semi-medium	2-4 ha	544	14	1,451	28
Medium	4-10 ha	156	4	864	17
Large	Above 10 ha	15	-	243	5
All sizes		3,966	100	5,144	100

Source: GoO 2005.

Table 6.7: Cost of cultivation and Crop Loan

Year / Particulars	1999-2000	2000-01	2001-02	2002-03	2003-04
Costs of cultivation of seasonal crops (Rs. crore)	3658	3375	4337	4642	5147
Crop loan (Rs. crore)	522	623	754	870	1107
% of costs of cultivation	14	18	17	19	22

owners nor the tillers take interest in this kind of business. Most importantly, among the farmers having larger landholdings also demand for term loan has remained low mainly because lack of mind-set to accept crop diversification, apprehensions about uncertainties in adopting hi-tech farming practices, unable to formulate economically viable and technically feasible land based schemes, etc. (Nayak, 2004).

As per a survey conducted by Orissa State Co-operative Bank (OSCB, 2004) out to about 50 lakh farm households (2001 census) only 9.08 lakh were using KCC issued by PACS/DCCBs for availing credit while another 3.40 lakh availed credit from nationalized banks and RRBs. The effective borrowers from all institutional sources in the farm sector may be thus around 12.47 lakh constituting only 25 per cent of the agricultural families in Orissa. If we consider the total ground level credit for farm sector goes only to these borrowers, then average per farmer agriculture credit during 2003-04 may be around Rs. 10,640 which is definitely a good sum of credit especially in a low productivity agricultural scenario like that of Orissa. Above all, only 2.04 lakh farmer families borrowed from non-institutional sources (OSCB, 2004).

Natural Calamities

During the last four decades of twentieth century Orissa witnessed as many as 31 abnormal years effected by floods, cyclones, droughts and other natural calamities causing maximum devastation in agriculture. Frequent occurrence of natural calamities perplexed farmers for large scale investments especially in agriculture sector.

Overdue and NPAs

Moreover, the default situation of a borrower from an institutional source restrains him/her to avail further credit from any banking institution. The low rate of recovery has remained a major concern for banks. About two thirds of the credit lent by Commercial Banks are overdue while the same for RRBs and DCCBs remained around half of the credit lent (Table 6.8) in past three years. Various studies and monitoring/inspections conducted by banks came out with the fact that willful default was also contributing to high rate of overdue. A higher rate of NPA and default accounts not only reduces the number of effective borrowers but also limits bankers from extending credit indiscriminately to a farmer. In order to make the repayment assured banks ask for higher collaterals and securities, which becomes difficult for many borrowers.

Table 6.8: Overdue and NPA Status of Banks in Orissa

(Percentage)

Agency	2002		2003		2004	
	Overdue	NPA	Overdue	NPA	Overdue	NPA
Commercial Banks	66	16	66	15	66	12
RRBs	46	16	48	18	49	25
OSCB	-	-	-	16	-	22
DCCBs	51	23	60	27	46	-
OSCARDB	82	100	94	100	-	67

Source: NABARD 2005.

CONCLUDING REMARKS

Institutional Credit is crucial for augmenting productivity and crop diversification and commercialization in agriculture. However, only one fourth of the farmers avail it. The reason is low effective demand for it from farmers. Various apprehensions of farmers for availing institutional credit and lack of mindset for application of modern farming practices and capital investment in agriculture put the effective demand for institutional credit at low. This minimized ground level credit flow to agriculture.

A few line of action may augment the effective demand as well as institutional credit flow in agriculture.

* Farmers in rural Orissa still have apprehensions in approaching banks for credit. Farmers must know that institutional credit is not at all a constraint to right kind of investments. Adequate education of farmers about institutional financing is warranted.
* Profitability in agriculture needs to be enhanced. Farmers have to be cultured for adoption of better technology and agrarian practices, switching over to high value crops and practicing precision farming.
* Location specific economically viable agricultural projects/schemes may be promoted. Agricultural graduates, consultants and researchers should design bankable schemes for effectuation.

* Orissa has vast unexploited surface in Central and Southern Hill Region, which is suitable for organic farming and export oriented crops. The progressive farmers in this region may be promoted to practice organic farming.
* Contract farming may be another area that can inspire people for crop diversification, commercialization and market linkages.
* Extension services for the development of agriculture and allied activities need be provided adequately. The government mechanisms as well as NGOs, Agricultural Universities/ graduates, etc. promote Research and Development activities for extension services as per the need.
* No doubt timely supply of credit by banks is important but timely repayment of loan by a borrower is more important. This enables to maintain a healthy and sustainable credit flow to the borrowers.

Central and State Governments play crucial role in rural credit through introduction of sponsored schemes, priority sector lending, subsidy linked programmes, etc. The farmers and entrepreneurs must take the advantage of it. The institutional framework has been putting forth all efforts for capacity building in quality supply of credit as well as popularizing schemes, banking plans and potential activities of reinvestment. However, banking sector alone may not be able to educate the entire gamut of farm and non-farm sector borrowers about various dimensions of institutional credit flow. It warrants concerted efforts from government and non-government organizations, every responsible citizen, researcher and educationist to educate the people about the advantages of institutional finance, capital formation in agriculture, crop diversification, commercialization in farming practices, schemes for agricultural and allied activities, and moreover to maintain a sustainable business relation with financing banks.

REFERENCES

Government of India, (2005), *Economic Survey 2004-05*, Economics Division, Ministry of Finance, New Delhi, India.

Government of Orissa, (2005), *Economic Survey 2004-05*, Directorate of Economics and Statistics, Planning and Coordination Department, Bhubaneswar, India.

NABARD, (2004), *Unit Cost of Farm Sector Investments for Orissa 2004-05*, National Bank for Agriculture and Rural Development, Orissa Regional Office, Bhubaneswar, Orissa, India.

Nayak, B. (2004), "Reviving Orissa Economy: The Areas for Structural Change." In: Raj Kishore Panda (Ed.), *Reviving Orissa Economy Opportunities and Areas of Action* APH Publishing Corporation, New Delhi, pp. 141-160.

Nayak, B. (2005), "Supply and Demand Aspects of Ground Level Institutional Credit Flow in Orissa." In: Raj Kishore Panda (Ed.), *Emerging Issues on Rural Credit*, A P H Publishing Corporation, New Delhi, pp. 209-227.

Orissa State Cooperative Bank, (2004), *Revitalisation of Cooperatives Through Member Contact - A Case Study of the Campaign Titled "Cooperatives at Your Doorstep"*, Bhubaneswar, Orissa, India.

Reserve Bank of India, (2004), *Report on Trend and Progress of Banking in India 2003-04*, Mumbai, India.

SFP, (1999), Orissa State Focus Paper 1999-2000, National Bank for Agriculture and Rural Development, Regional Office, Bhubaneswar, India.

SFP, (2002), Orissa State Focus Paper 2002-2003, National Bank for Agriculture and Rural Development, Regional Office, Bhubaneswar, India.

SFP, (2005), Orissa State Focus Paper 2005-2006, National Bank for Agriculture and Rural Development, Orissa Regional Office, Bhubaneswar, India.

Financial Derivative After Globalisation

—*Sudhir Pradhan**
—*Biswanath Patro***

INTRODUCTION

Derivative is a financial asset which derives its value from some specified underlying asset. In finance, a security whose price is dependent upon or derived form one or more underlying assets. The derivative itself is merely a contract between two or more parties. Its value is determined by fluctuations in the underlying asset. The most common underlying assets include stocks, bonds, commodities, currencies, interest rates and market indexes. Most derivatives are characterized by high leverage. Something derived, it means that something have to be derived or arisen out of the underlying variables. For example, financial derivative is an instrument indeed derived from the financial market.

* MBA, Finance, doing Ph.D. under the guidance of Dr. R.N. Misra, Prof MBA, SMIT, Ankushpan (under B.P.U.T.)

** Faculty Member, PGCMS, SMIT, Berhampur.

The limit of the ratio of the change is a function to the corresponding change in its independent variable. This explains that the value of financial derivative will change as per the change in the value of the underlying financial instrument. Derivatives are structurally related to other substances. In case of financial derivatives, they are derived for a combination of cash market instruments or other derivative instruments.

The term "Derivative" indicates that it has no independent value, i.e., its value is entirely derived from the value of the underlying asset. The underlying assets can be securities, commodities, bullion, currency live stock or anything else. In other words, derivative means forward, futures, option or any other hybrid contract or predetermined fixed duration linked for the purpose of contract fulfillment to the value of a specified real or financial asset or to an index of securities.

What the above definition conveys that, the derivatives are financial products. Derivative is derived from another financial instrument/contract called the underlying.

OBJECTIVE AND SCOPE OF THE STUDY

For the purpose of the study, only Financial derivative has been taken into consideration. The secondary data published in books, journals, magazines, daily papers, periodicals are uses in this study so all the limitations of secondary data are available in this data.

CLASSIFICATION OF FINANCIAL DERIVATIVE

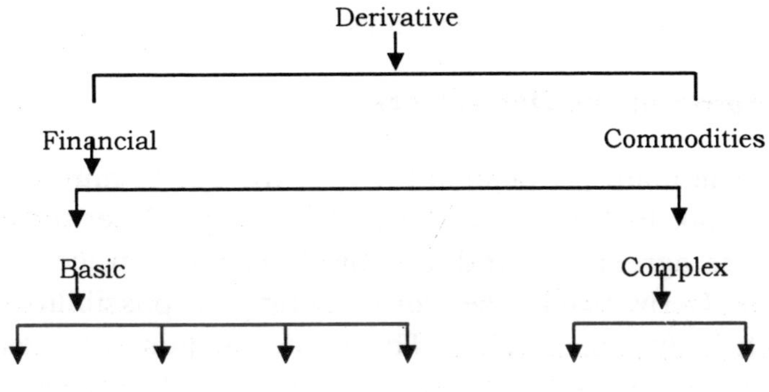

Forward Futures Options Warrants & Convertibles Swaps Exotics (Non-standard)

(Classification of Derivatives)

One form of classification of derivative instruments is between commodity derivatives and financial derivatives. The basic difference between these is the nature of the underlying instrument or asset.

TYPES OF DERIVATIVES

1. **Commodity derivative:** The underlying instrument is a commodity which may be wheat, cotton, pepper, sugar, jute, turmeric, corn, soybeans, crude oil, natural gas, gold, silver, copper and so on.
2. **Financial derivative:** In a financial derivative, the underlying instrument may be treasury bills, stocks, bonds, foreign exchange, stock index, guilt-edged securities, cost of living index etc. It is to be noted that financial derivate is fairly

standard and there are no quality issues where as in commodity derivative, the quality may be the underlying matters.

Purpose of the Derivatives

The main purpose of the derivative is to minimize our risk in future market, which is predetermined before agreement and at a predetermined price and time. Derivative is used for hedging pour possibility of risk in future market. The basic purpose of these instruments is to provide commitments to prices for future dates for giving protection against adverse movement in future prices, in order to reduce the extent of financial risks. Not only this, they also provide opportunities to earn profit for those persons who are ready to for higher risks. In other words, these instruments, indeed, facilities to transfer the risk from those who wish to avoid in to those who are willing to accept the same.

The total derivative market is depends on the underlying asset. According to the quality of the asset determines the agreement and it makes very strong.

Components of Derivative

For the agreements of derivative market there some requirements which will make the agreement very strong. These components are:

- Two persons or any financial institutions
- Underlying asset.
- Predetermined time.

- Predetermined price and place.
- Clearing corporation.

Feature of a Financial Derivative

As observed earlier, a financial derivative is a financial instrument whose value is derived from the value of an underlying asset; hence the name "Derivative" came to existence.

The basic features of the derivative instrument can be drawn from the general definition of a derivative irrespective of its type. Derivatives or derivative securities are future contracts which are written between two parties (Counter Parties) and whose value are derived from the value of underlying widely held and easily marketable assets such as agricultural and other physical (Tangible) commodities, or short-term or long-term financial instruments, or intangible things like weather, commodities price index (inflation rate), equity price index, bond price index, stock market index, etc.:

A. A derivative instrument related to the future contract between two parties. It means there must be a contract binding on the underlying parties and the same to be fulfilled in future. The future period short-term or long-term depends upon the nature or contract, for example, short-term interest rate futures and long-term interest rate futures contract.

B. In general, the counter parties have specified obligation under the derivative contract. Obviously, the nature of the obligation would be different as per the type of the instrument of a derivative. For example, the obligation of the counter parties, under the different derivatives, such as formal contracts, future contract, option contract and Swap contract would be different.

C. The derivative contract can be undertaken directly between the two parties or through the particular exchange like financial futures contracts. The exchange traded derivates are quite liquid and have low transaction costs in comparison to tailor made contracts, e.g., Exchange derivatives are DOWJONES, NIFTY, BSE, NSE, MIDEX, SIMEX, and HONGSENG.

D. The financial derivatives are carried balance sheet. The size of the derivative is contract depends upon its notional amount. The notional amount is the amount used to calculate the payoff.

E. Usually, in derivatives, trading, the taking or making of delivery of underlying assets is not involved; rather underlying transactions are mostly settled by taking off setting positions in the derivatives themselves. There is, therefore, no effective limit on the quantity of claims, which can be traded in respect of underlying assets.

F. Although in the market, general exchange traded derivatives are being increasing evolved in privately negotiated customized, over the counter (OTC) traded derivatives are existence. They expose the trading parties to operational risk, counter party risk and legal risk.

G. Financial the derivative instruments, sometimes, because of their off-balance sheet nature, can be used to clear up the balance sheet.

HISTORY OF DERIVATIVES MARKETS

Historically, it is evidently that the development of futures markets followed the development of forward markets. It is believed that the forward trading has been in existence since 12th century in England and France. Forward trading in rice was started in 17th century in Japan; know as *Cho-at-Mai* a king (rice trade-on-book) concentrated around Dojima in Osaka, later on the trade in rice grew with a high degree of standardization. In 1730, this market got official recognition form the Tokugawa Shogurate. As such, the Dojima rice market became the first futures market in the sense that is was registered on organized exchange with the standardized exchange with the standardized trading norms.

The International Monetary Market was formed as division of the *Chicago Mercantile Exchange* in 1972 for futures trading in foreign currencies. The basic use of forward trading was to cover the price risk. In earlier years, transporting goods from one market to other markets took many months. For e.g., in the 1800 food grains produced in *England* sent through ships to the *United States* which normally took few months. Sometimes, during this time, the price crashed due to unfavourable events before the goods reached to the destination. In such cases, the producers had to sell their goods at the loss. Therefore, the produces sought to avoid such price risk by selling their goods forward, or on a "to arrive" basis. The basic idea behind this move at that time was simply to cover future price risk.

On the opposite side, the speculator or other commercial firms seeking to offset their price risk came forward to go for such trading. In this way, the forward trading in commodities came into existence. Although financial derivatives have been in operation since long, but they have become a major force in financial markets in the early 1970s.

Hence, the first financial futures market was the International Monetary Market, established in 1972 by the *Chicago Mercantile Exchange* which was followed by the *London International financial Futures Exchange* in 1982.

Commodities futures trading was initiated long back in 1950s, however, the 1960s marked a period of great decline in futures trading. Market after market was closed usually because different commodities' prices increases were attributed to speculation on these markets. Accordingly, the Central Government imposed the ban on trading in derivatives in 1969 under a notification issue. The late 1990s shows this signs of opposite trends - a large scale revival of futures markets in India, and hence, the Central Government revoked the ban on futures trading in October, 1995. The Civil Supplies Ministry agreed in principle for starting of futures trading in Basmati rice, further, in 1996 the Government granted permission to the Indian Pepper and Spice Trade Association to convert its Pepper Futures Exchange into an International Pepper Exchange. As such, on November 17, 1997, India's first international futures exchange at Kochi, Known as the India Pepper and Spice Trade Association-International Commodity Exchange (IPSTA-ICE) was established. Similarly, the Cochi Oil Millers

Association, in June 1996, demanded the introduction of futures trading in coconut oils. The Central Minister for Agriculture announced in June 1996 that he was in favours of introduction of futures trading both domestic and international. Further, a new coffee futures exchange (the Coffee Futures Exchange of India) is being started at Bangalore. In August, 1997, the Central Government proposed that Indian companies with commodity price exposures should be allowed to use foreign futures and option markets. The trend is not confined to the commodity markets alone, it has initiated in financial futures too.

The RBI set up the Sodhani Expert Group which recommended major liberalization of the forward exchange market and had urged the setting up of rupee-based derivatives in financial instruments. The RBI accepted several of its recommendations in August, 1996. A landmark step taken in this regard when the SEBI appointed a Committee named the Dr. L.C. Gupta Committee (LCGC) by its resolution, dated November 18, 1996 in order to develop appropriate regulatory framework for derivatives trading in India. While the Committee's focus was on equity derivatives but it had maintained a board perspective of derivative in general. The Board of SEBI, on May 11, 1998 accepted the recommendations of the Dr. L.C. Gupta Committee and approved introduction of derivatives trading in India in the phased manner. Accordingly, in December, 1999, the new framework has been approved and 'Derivatives' have been accorded the status of 'Securities'. In June, 2000, the National Stock Exchange and the Bombay Stock Exchange started stock index based futures trading in

India. This is mainly attributed to the low awareness about the product and mechanism among the market players and investors. The volumes, however, are gradually picking up due to active interest of the institutional investors.

Financial Derivatives in India

Forward Contract

A. A forward contract is a simple customized contract between two parties to buy or sell an asset at a certain time in the future for a certain price.

B. Forward contracts are Bilateral contract (the contract made between the two parties), and hence, they are expose to counter-party risk. There is risk of non-performance of obligation either of the parties, so these are riskier than to future contracts.

C. Each contract is custom designed, they decided about the terms and condition like contract size, date of agreement, the asset type, quality, etc.

D. A forward contract is an agreement between two parties to buy or sell an asset at a future date at a price agreed today. So, in case of forward contract, the date, the price rate, and the quantity, all are decided at the contract date, but the contract is implemented in future on the agreed date.

E. The buyer and the seller they already decided to buy and the counter party sell that asset at a specified future date and at a same specified price.

F. The forward contract the counter party who buy or sells the asset they can take the help of hedging process because to decrease the risk in forward contract.

G. The forward price for a particular forward contract at a particular time is the deliver price.

H. It is important to differentiate between the forward price and the delivery price. However, as time passes, the forward price is likely to change whereas the delivery price remains the same.

I. In the forward contract, derivative assets can often be contracted from the combination of underlying assets, such assets are often known as synthetic assets in the forward market.

J. Actually in Indian forward market the contract maximum period is 90 days within that period both the parties to buy or sell the asset at certain specified period at a forward price.

K. In case the party wishes to cancel the contract, it has to compulsory go to the same counter party. The cancellation will do by the NATIONAL STOCK CLEARING CORPORATION LIMITED.

L. The cancellation will take place, who wish to cancel the agreement or contract, who will bear the loss and he bound to pay the penalty to the counter party at NSCC.

M. The cancellation takes place because of the stock index fluctuation. The stock market increases sometimes and sometimes it declines. The market condition the demand and supply will affect in the forward market. If there is any change in supply then ultimately it effects in demand. If supply decreases the demand increases and the stock market index increases and the supply is more than the demand the stock index declines. Hence, the agreement or the contract forward price value fluctuates and the cancellation takes place:

- After the cancellation the agreement is newly another contract will made by both the parties for the same asset.
- The parties may contract as per their own requirement and suitability. So, the forward contracts are generally tailor-made.

If brief, a forward contract is an agreement between the counter parties to buy or sell a specified quantity of an asset at a specified price, with delivery at a specified time (future) and place. These contracts are not standardized; each one is usually being customized to its owner's specification.

FUTURE CONTRACT

A future contract is an agreement between two parties to buy or sell a specified quantity of an asset at a specified price and at a specified time and place. Future contracts are normally traded in an exchange which sets the certain standardized norms for trading in futures contracts.

Standardization

One of the most important features of future

contract is that the contract has certain standardized specification i.e., quality of the asset, quantity of the asset, the date and month of delivery, the units of price quotation, location and settlement place.

Clearing Corporation

In the future contract, the stock exchange acts as an intermediary or middlemen in futures. It gives the guarantee for the performance of the parties to each transaction. Thus clearing house is a counter party in this contract. The stock exchange provides them transparency, liquidity, anonymity of trades, and also eliminates the counter party risks due to the guarantee provided by Nation Securities Clearing Corporation Limited. (NSCCL).

The futures are the transferable future delivery contacts. Both the parties to the futures have a right to transfer the contract by entering into offsetting future contract. If not transferred specified date, then they have obligations to fulfill the terms and conditions of the contract.

Daily Settlement and Margin/Stock Broker

When a person enters into the future contract he must invest to deposit fund with broker, which is called margin. The broker can set higher margin for his client. The stock broker protects from risk to his client.

Tick Size

The futures are expressed in currency units; with a minimum price movement is called a tick size.

Cash Settlement

Most of the contracts is settled in cash by having the short or long-term. The expiration date is most important.

Delivery

The future contracts are executed on the expiry date. The counter party to make delivery with in that date and it is the obligation for their contract.

Futures are like liquid forward contracts. Future as a technique of risk management, provide several services to the investors and speculators.

Options Contracts

Options are most important group of derivatives securities. Option may be defined as a contract, between two parties whereby one party obtains the right, but not the obligation, to buy or sell a particular asset, at a specified price, on or before a specified date.

- The person who acquires the right is known as option buyer or option holder.
- While the other person (who confers the right) is known as option seller or option writer.
- There are two types of options. (1) The call potion and (2) The put option.
- *The call option:* A call option provides to the holder a right to buy specified assets at specified price on or before a specified data.

- *The put option:* a put potion provides to the holder a right to sell specified assets at specified price on or before a specified date.
- The specified price in such contract is known as the exercise price or the strike price.
- The date in the contract is known as the expiration date or exercise date or the maturity date.
- The asset or security instrument or commodity covered under the contract is called as the underlying asset.
- *Option premium*: In options, the buyer of the option has to buy the right from the seller by paying an option premium.
- The amount of option premium depends upon the strike rate, the duration of the option period and volatility of price of the underlying asset.
- Obviously the call option is higher at lower strike price and lower at higher price.
- The put option premium is higher at higher strike price and lower at lower strike price.
- In India all options are available for a period of one month, two month or three month. All these options end on the last Thursday of a calendar month, e.g., if a person option took, during the month of January for one, two or three months shall expire on the last Thursday of January, February and March Respectively.
- Those options have been offers in Sensex, **Satyam, Reliance, SBI and Tata Steel**. These options expire every week on Friday.

WARRANTS

Warrants is just like an option contract where the holder has the right to buy shares of a specified company at a certain price during the given time period. In other words, the folder of a warrant instrument has the right to purchase a specific number of shares at a fixed price in a fixed period from a issuing company:

- ❖ If the holder exercises the right or purchases more and more shares then it increases the number of shares of the issuing company.
- ❖ Warrants are issued as sweeteners attached senior securities like bonds and debentures. So that they are, those companies issues equities that they are successful in their equity issues in terms of volume and price.
- ❖ Warrants can be detached and traded separately.
- ❖ Warrants are highly speculative and leverage instruments.

CONVERTIBLES

Convertibles are hybrid securities which combine the basic attributes of fixed interest and variable return securities.

- ❖ Most popular among the convertible hybrid securities are convertible bonds, convertible debentures, and convertible preference shares.
- ❖ These securities are called equity derivative securities.

- These hybrid securities are fully converted into equity shares of the issuing company.
- These terms differ from Company as per nature of the instrument and particular equity issue of the company.

SWAP

In finance, a swap is a derivative in which two counter parties agree to exchange one stream of cash flows against another stream. These streams are called legs of the swap.

The cash flows are calculated over a notional principal amount, which is usually not exchanged between counterparties.

Swaps can be used to hedge certain risks such as interest risk or to speculate on changes in the underlying prices.

CONCLUSION

Use of Derivatives

- One of the most important services provided by the derivatives is to control, avoid, shift and manage efficiently different types of risks through various strategies like hedging, arbitraging, spreading, etc. Derivatives assist the holders to shift or modify suitably the risk characteristics of their portfolios. These are specifically useful in highly volatile financial market conditions like erratic trading, highly flexible interest rates, volatile exchange rates and monetary chaos.

- Derivatives serve as barometers of the future trends in prides which result in the discovery of new prices both on the spot and futures markets. Further, they help in disseminating different new prides both on the spot and futures markets trading of various commodities and securities to the society which enable to discover or form suitable correct or true equilibrium prices in the markets. As a result, they assist in appropriate and superior allocation of resources in the society.
- As we see that in derivatives trading no immediate full amount of the transaction is required since most of them are based on margin trading. As a result, large number of traders, speculators arbitrageurs operate in such markets. So, derivatives trading enhance liquidity and reduce transaction costs in the markets for underlying assets.
- The derivatives assist the investors, traders and managers or large pools of funds to devise such strategies so that they may make proper asset allocation increase their yields and achieve other investment goals.
- It has been observed from the derivatives trading in the market that the derivatives have smoothen out price fluctuations, squeeze the price spread, integrate price structure at different points of time and remove gluts and shortages in the markets.
- The derivatives trading encourage the competitive trading in the markets, different risk

taking preference of the market operators like speculator, hedgers, traders, arbitrageurs, etc. resulting in increase in trading volume in the country. They also attract young investors, professionals and other experts who will act as catalysts to the growth of financial markets.

- Lastly, it is observed that derivatives trading develop the market towards 'complete markets'. Complete market concept refers to that situation where no particular investors be better of than others, or patterns of returns of all additional securities are spanned by the already existing securities in it, or there is no further scope of additional security.

REFERENCES

Gordon, E., *Financial Markets and Service*, Himalaya Publishing House, New Delhi, 2007.

Gupta. S.L., *Financial Derivatives*, Printice-Hall of India Private Limited, New Delhi, 2007.

Changing Pattern of Panchayat Finance in Orissa: A Study

*—Dr. Bhagabata Patro**

*—Dr. Kishore Chandra Pattnaik***

*—Bibhu Prasad Sahu****

Orissa continuous to remain poor in spite of abundant natural resources probably due to poor governance, absence of a dynamic leadership and also with regard to institutional arrangement of governance. The role of PR institutions in the state has been minimal since the state became a separate province in 1936. Whatever little decentralization appeared in the state is perhaps due to the pressure arising out of national level policies to strengthen the local self-government in the country. It is admitted by the State Finance Commission that theoretically the local self-government is strong in Orissa but not in practice (First SFC, 1998).

* Reader in Economics, Berhampur University.

** Senior Lecturer in Economics, City College, Berhampur.

*** Senior Researcher, Centre for Local Government Budget and Policy Research, YSD, Berhampur.

ORGANIZATIONAL STRUCTURE OF PRIS

The most important obstacle in strengthening the rural local bodies in Orissa is the absence of political will with the state government officials and legislators to share power with the local government functionaries. Before 73rd constitutional amendment, the PRIs appeared and disappeared at the mercy of the state government. Elections were held after much delay every time and the government suspends the elected bodies very frequently on some pretext or other. Elaborate taxing powers were given to the Gram Panchayat but were sparingly used by the local government to generate internal resources.

After independence, the Orissa Gram Panchayat Act, 1948 passed to facilitate decentralized administration in the state.

The Panchayat were entrusted to discharge developmental civil and judicial functions. The reconstitution of Gram Panchayat was made so as to ensure a minimum annual income of Rs. 2500 per Panchayat and population coverage between 5000 to 10000. By 1953-54, out of 46992 villages (1971 census) only 20906 villages i.e. less than 50% were covered by Gram Panchayat. The Orissa Gram Panchayat Act, 1964 was passed to entrust specific functions to the GPs. By 1967, they were 3830 Panchayats in the state with around 5000 population per Panchayat. (Rao, 1983) The GPs were entrusted the functions of street lighting, sanitation, drainage, water supply etc. After introduction of Community Development Programme and National Extension Services in the country during first plan the state created C.D. Blocks. Panchayat Samities and Zilla Parishad came in to existence in 1961 to promote further decentralization at the middle level. In 1968, the Zilla Parishads were abolished, as they were found not useful for executing development programmes. However the role of Panchayat Samities has gained importance over the years and they were entrusted to implement many state government responsibilities at the grass-root level. The emergence of PSs as implementing agencies of the state has created some confusion with regard to their role as an independent local government unit. This tier of the PRIs has no resources of their own and in choosing the appropriate level of public service they have limited independence. The functions entrusted to Panchayat Samities were planning, execution and supervision of development programme, management and control of primary education, trusts and endowments, vaccination and registration of births and deaths. The functions discharged were mostly of delegated type and implemented as per the guideline of state and central government. A set of new acts were passed by the state government in 1991 to revitalize the PRIs under the leadership of the then Chief Minister Sri Biju Pattnaik. These acts were again amended to have conformity with provisions of constitutional amendments in 1993. (Jena, 2003) The Zilla Parishads were revived in 1997 and were appended to the District Rural Development Agencies. The present responsibilities of ZPs are mostly to co-ordinate the activities of the line departments of the state government at the district level. The Government of Orissa has recently proposed to transfer a part of administration of 11 items to the PRIs fold but not succeeded fully till now. At present a three-tier PRI system is in operation in Orissa with 6234 GPs, 314 PSs and 30ZPs (SSFC, 2004).

PLAN PROPOSAL TO STRENGTHEN PRIs

A glimpse of the plan document of the State reflects that up to the Seventh Plan the emphasis was on the development of Block Panchayat and Gram Panchayat by designing specific programmes. The Block Panchayats were conceived as grass-root administration units and a well designed administrative structure is provided for this. The Block Development Officer, a state government bureaucrat is assigned the task of being the chief executive of a block working under the block Chairmen, an elected representative. However, the normal practice is the domination of the local MLAs in the decision making process in a block as he is present in all the meetings of the PS. If the MLA belongs to the same political party that of the Chairman then the developmental programmes work smoothly. Otherwise there is always tussle between the two with regard to selection of beneficiary/schemes under different government programmes. Specific schemes for PRIs came into existence in the Fourth Plan these were:

- Construction of Panchayat Ghars.
- Construction and improvement of roads.
- Loans for developing markets.
- Construction of grain goals.

The total expenditure incurred in the Fourth Plan for all these purposes was Rs. 18.4 lakhs and it was distributed among 3800 Gram Panchayats in the state.

The per capital allocation for a Panchayat thus comes to Rs. 500 in 1967 (Fourth plan). The power of Gram Panchayats to impose panchayat tax, vehicle tax and professional tax was withdrawn and these resulted in reduced internal resource mobilization of Gram Panchayats. The Fifth Plan objective was to augment the resources of Panchayats and develop them as self sustained units. For this purpose it was envisaged to transfer the control and management of few public properties and extend loan finance to these institutions. The State Government has proposed expenditure of Rs. 180 lakhs for the Fifth Plan period. The activities promoted were construction of Panchayat ghars, training of Panchayat secretaries and incentive grant to the Gram Panchayats.

The Sixth Plan allocation for GPs was Rs. 400 lakhs and the activities covered were almost the same. Maintenance and improvement of village orchards has emerged as an important scheme in this plan and a sum of Rs. 24 lakhs was allotted as grant-in-aid for this purpose. The Seventh Plan allocation to Panchayats has witnessed substantial reduction and reached a figure of Rs. 150 lakhs for the entire period. In the Eighth Plan the chapter on Panchayat was deleted reflecting least priority of the government to PRIs in the planning mechanism of the state.

ELEVENTH FINANCE COMMISSION/STATE FINANCE COMMISSION GRANTS AND PRIs

The recommendations of the Eleventh Finance Commission (EFC), the First State Finance Commission (SFC) and the Second State Finance Commission have brought slight change in the resource and activity position of the Panchayatiraj bodies in the State. This paper is an attempt to analyze the principles followed in the distribution of EFC grants, the extent of its impact and the improvement in the financial position of Panchayats and the developmental impact on certain Panchayats in the state.

METHODOLOGY

To examine the hypothesis stated above, the methodology adopted is to see the distribution of EFC grant at the district level and the utilization thereof with the help of secondary data available in the office of the District Panchayat Officer (DPO). The final impact of the EFC/SFC grant on Gram Panchayat is also simultaneously examined by analyzing the finance position of a particular Gram Panchayat which is collected from the official record of that Panchayat. The analysis has not covered the situation of the PSs and Zilla Panchayats.

ELEVENTH FINANCE COMMISSION GRANTS AT THE DISTRICT LEVEL

Information collected from the office of the DPO, Ganjam, reveals that the Government of Orissa released the first installment of EFC grants meant for 2000-2001 in the year 2001-2002 and grant meant for 2001-2002 in June 2003. The criterion of distribution was on the basis of population of Gram Panchayat. This is given in the Table 8.1.

On this basis the 22 blocks of the district got their respective shares for the financial year of 2001-02. The DPO, Ganjam received a sum of Rs. 5.20 crore of

01-02 and Rs. 4.83 crore for the year 2001-02 from the government. The block-wise distribution is presented in Table 8.2.

Table 8.1: Criteria of Distribution of EFC grant

(amount in Rs.)

Population	Amount
<5000	1,05,000.00
5000-7000	1,20,000.00
7000-10000	1,25,000.00
>10000	1,00,000.00

Source: *Official records of the District Panchayat Officer, Ganjam, Orissa.*

Table 8.2: Distribution of EFC Grants to Blocks in Ganjam District for the Years 2000-2002

(Rs. in thousand)

Name of the Block	2000-2001	2001-2002
Chatrapur	2160	1885
Ganjam	1550	1440
Khalikote	2895	2635
Beguniapada	2470	2210
Polasara	2745	2560
Purusottampur	2765	2510
Kabisurya Nagar	2055	2040
Hinjilicut	2305	2115
Rangeilunda	2530	2460
Patrapur	2620	2340
Chikiti	1890	1730
Digapahandi	2725	2465
Kukudakhandi	2395	2080
Sanakhemundi	2500	2255
Bhanjanagar	2370	2075
Belaguntha	2095	1865

Name of the Block	2000-2001	2001-2002
Jagnnathprasad	2685	2405
Buguda	1955	2010
Aska	2960	2645
Dharakote	1885	1750
Sorada	2230	2495
Sheragada	2285	2200
Total	52070	48320

Source: *Official Records of the District Panchayat Officer, Ganjam Orissa.*

Another important dimension of EFC grants is the extent of utilization by the GPs in the State as on 2004. For Ganjam district, information on this is only available for few blocks. The money allocated for the year 2000-2001 is reported to be utilized to the extent of 76 per cent in these blocks. There exists wide variation among the blocks with regard to the pattern of utilization. Only nine out of the 22 blocks of the district have submitted their utilization certificate at the time of this study. Some blocks of the district like Patrapur and Aska reported more than 95 per cent utilization whereas for Rangeilunda block, a block adjacent to Berhampur city it is only 28 per cent. All this explained in the Table 8.3.

To understand the utilization pattern of EFC grants at the lowest level, the study examined the financial transaction of a single Gram Panchayat. The name of the GP identified is "Dura" which is located at a distance of around five km, from Berhampur city. The GP consists of a total population of around eight thousand and has five villages.

Table 8.3: Pattern of Utilization of EFC grants in selected blocks during the year 2000-2001

(Rupees in thousands)

Name of the Block	Amount released	Amount spent	Balance	Percent age of utilization
Kabisurya Nagar	2055	1273	782	62
Rangeilunda	2530	710	1820	28
Patrapur	2620	2568	52	98
Kukudakhandi	2395	1990	405	83
Chikiti	1890	1726	163	91
Sorada	2230	1258	971	56
Sheragada	2285	1712	572	75
Aska	2960	2835	125	96
Belaguntha	2095	1852	242	88
Total	21060	15942	5118	76

Source: *Official Records of the Districts Panchayat officer, Ganjam, Orissa.*

EFC GRANTS AT THE GRAM PANCHAYAT LEVEL

The Panchayat has sizable population working in the government sector and thus is economically in a very sound position. Farming is the other prominent occupation of the people in this Panchayat. The Secretary of the Panchayats reported that he has received the EFC grant only for one year i.e. for 2000-2001 amounting Rs. 1.42 lakhs. Out of this the expenditure incurred is as given in Table 8.4.

The data reveals highest percentage of expenditure in water supply and sanitation activities followed by the public conveniences. Primary health care got least priority and its share was five per cent only.

Table 8.4: Detailed Expenditure pattern of EFC grant of 'Dura' Gram Panchayat for 2000-2001

(In Rupees)

Item	Amount Spent	Percentage of the Total
Primary Education	26008	19
Primary Health	7060	5
Water Supply and Sanitation	46235	34
Public Conveniences	31149	23
Streetlight	27300	19
Total	137752	100

Source: Official records of Dura Gram Panchayat, Dura.

SFC RECOMMENDATION AND PANCHAYAT FINANCES

In Orissa, the First SFC was constituted in the year 1998, just before the arrival of the National Finance Commission to estimate the requirements of funds for the local governments. The Commission examined the situation and stated that developing the local governments by devolution of funds from consolidated fund of the State is impossible due to financial crisis of the State Government. However the commission expressed its displeasure for not releasing the state's share of the EFC grant. The Commission also expressed its happiness in high irregularity in case of payment of local government share from cess on land revenue and grant out of *kendu* leaf profit.

Examination of financial position of a specific Panchayat for a period of a four year reveals that the income of the Panchayat is still dominated by grants from the State Government and Central Government.

The income of the Panchayat is given in Table 8.5. The grants for JGSY and SGSY are not included in the income and expenditure side of this analysis. The income from own tax has not shown any significant change over the period. It is around 4% of the total revenue for the whole period. Non-tax revenue however, has increased in the first three years revealing good potential in it. Grants-in-aid continuous to claim the highest share throughout the period and depicts an uneven trend. For the first three years, there is declining trend but thereafter in 2002-03, it increased to 85 per cent.

On the expenditure front salary component consumes more than three-fourth of the total. Development works has never entered a double digit figure. All other expenditure items have no definite trend.

CONCLUSION AND POLICY SUGGESTIONS

The following are the conclusions and policy suggestions that can be deduced from the analysis carried out in the earlier paragraphs:

- The financial position of the GPs shows that there is no effort to mobilize own resources. So while fixing the criteria of distribution it is necessary that the grants from the upper tier be linked to a minimum quantum of own resources to be mobilized by the PRI bodies.
- To counter horizontal equity in the application of the principle given above, it is necessary to develop some criteria of identifying the backwardness of a PRI unit and follow a

Table 8.5: Income of Dura Gram Panchayat for the period 1999-00 to 2002-03

(in Rupees)

Item	1999-2000	2000-01	2001-02	2002-03
Salary	41674 (78.5)	39943 (75.4)	47404 (88.7)	50413 (82.6)
Development Works	270 (0.5)	4000 (7.6)	-	3986 (6.5)
TA and DA	3010 (5.7)	3320 (6.3)	2270 (4.2)	910 (1.5)
Telephone and Electricity	1696 (3.2)	2950 (5.6)	1815 (3.4)	460 (0.7)
Misc.	6450 (12.2)	2760 (5.2)	1971 (3.7)	5262 (8.6)
Total	53040	52974	53460	61031

Source: Official Records of Dura Gram Panchayat, Dura.

principle to uplift the lagged backward region PRIs.

- It is noticed that the infrastructure base of the GPs was very poor. Even the existing infrastructure facilities remain unutilized due to inability of the GP to pay for the recurring expenses associated to maintain these assets. For example, in case of streetlights (an item recommended by FCS) the GP is unable to pay the power tariff due to poor collection from the people. So while providing for maintenance costs, of some assets it should be made mandatory that assets be in an used condition and the villagers are ready to bear the recurring costs associated with the asset.

- Analysis of the financial devolution of the rural local bodies, particularly Gram Panchayats in Orissa reveals predominance of central government grants the State Government grants are shrinking over the years. This also means, while formulating the future devolution schemes, the National Finance Commission, should link to a maintain amount of matching share from the State Government.

- The most important confusion with regards to empowering the local government relates to allowing them to act independently with assured resources base at their command. The present field situation is that the middle and upper tier of the PRI bodies do not have their own resource of revenue and depend on the state. The State Dovernment also uses these bodies as the agent of the State to implement various development programmes. In the block, the MLA decides virtually everything. The discretion of the local government functionaries is severely limited because of this.

REFERENCES

Economic Survey, 2002-03, Government of Orissa, Director of Economics and Statistics, Bhubaneswar.

First Report of the Second Finance Commission, Bhubaneswar, 2003.

Jena, A.C., *Devolution of Functions and Finances of Panchayats in Orissa,* NIRD, Hyderabad, 2003.

Manual of Panchayatiraj Institutions, Legal Miscellany, Cuttack

Rao, K.V. Narayana, *Finances of Panchayati Raj in Orissa,* National Institute of Rural Development, Hyderabad, 1983.

Report of the Eleventh Finance Commission, 2000-05, New Delhi.

Report of the First State Finance Commission, (Chairman Prof. Baidyanath Mishra, Bhubaneswar, 1998).

Report of the Second State Finance Commission, Orissa, 2004.

Management of Financial Services in Orissa – A Look

—*Dr. Anil Kumar Sahu**

FINANCIAL SERVICES IN ORISSA

In any Economy, Money is at the core of each and every type of financial services. Whether developed or underdeveloped. Financial services help in fully tackling and explaining the complete functioning of the financial market the world over.

The word "finance" means funds of monetary resources required by various entities the individuals, business, corporations and Government. As rapid economic growth the Indian Banking System under gone a dynamic change during the post national-itisation period i.e. from 1969.

It became any important institutions for most efficient utilization of the economy, it augments its saving the vast network of financial institutions has emerged particularly it rural areas in the country. The

* Reader in MBA Department, Berhampur University, Orissa.

financial services of banking sector has been a phenomenon growth, Commercial Banks directed to open large number of rural and saving urban branches and have shouldered the responsibility for mobility the public savings for developing the economic of the state of Orissa.

FINANCIAL SERVICES IN INDIA

Financial services broadly incorporate the system of borrowing and learning of funds, the financial services included the demand and supply of all different individual companies, institution, corporation and Government this are agriculture finance, industrial finance, development finance and government finance.

Chart I: The Indian Banking System

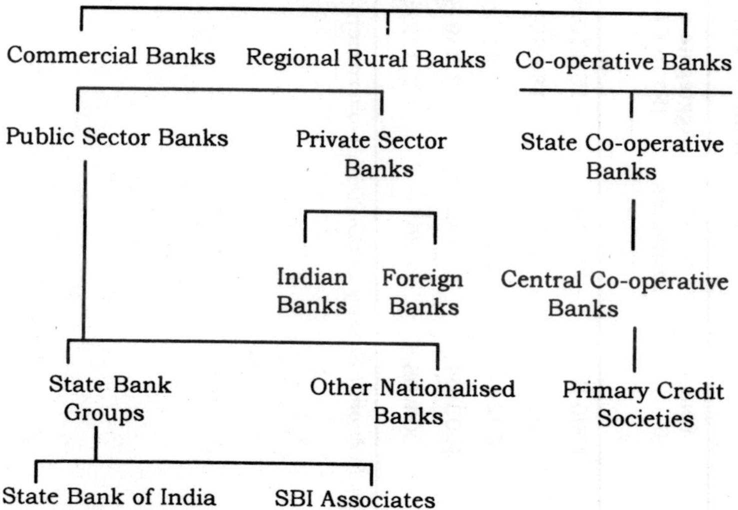

Table 9.1: Performance of all Scheduled Commercial Banks in Orissa

Sl. No.	Year	No. of Branches	Aggregate deposit (Rs in Crore)	Gross Bank credits (Rs. in crore)	Credit deposit ratio	Population per branch (in thousand)
1.	2000-01	2,214	15,110.87	6,264.98	41.46	16.6
2.	2001-02	2,224	18,689.18	8,527.15	45.63	16.6
3.	2002-03	2,232	20,347.87	10,430.71	51.26	16.6
4.	2003-04	2,242	23,359.86	13,390.53	57.32	17.0
5.	2004-05	2,261	27,372.64	17,587.83	64.25	17.0

Source: Economy Survey 2005-2006, Government of Orissa, Bhubaneswar.

Table 9.1 shows that during 2004-05, the total deposits with these commercial banks were of the order of Rs. 27,372.64 crore as against Rs. 23, 359.86 crore during 2003-04 and the total advances made by these Commercial Banks were Rs. 17,587.83 crore as against Rs. 13, 390.53 crore during 2003-04. The credit deposit ration has increased fro, 41.46 in 2000-01 to 64.25 in 2004-05, which is, however, less than the all India average of 66.04 in 2004-05.

Table 9.2 shows that, during 2003-04, there were 1,394 branches of Public sector banks in the State which increased to 1,408 during 2004-05. During 2004-05, deposits in these banks were of the order of Rs. 23, 041.08 crore and total advances were Rs.14,874.98 crore as against Rs.19,462.10 crore deposits and Rs.11,320.87 crore advances during 2003-04. The credit-deposit ratio, which was 58.17 in 2003-04, has increased to 64.56 during 2004-05. During 2004-05, the total advances made by the public sector commercial banks to Agricultural sector were Rs. 1,632.05 crore to SSI sector Rs.1,094.81 crore, Services sector Rs. 5,444.29 crore and to S.C. and S.T. were Rs. 980.82 crore.

Table 9.2: Deposit and Advance made by different Banks in Orissa (As on 31-3-2005)

(Rs. in lakh)

Sl. No.	Name of Bank	No. of Branches	Total Deposit	Total Advance
1	2	3	4	5
1.	Allahabad Bank	63	92167	67637
2.	Andhra Bank	79	104180	50170
3.	Bank of Baroda	36	34193	31581
4.	Bank of India	115	117035	97128

(contd.)

1	2	3	4	5
5.	Bank of Maharashtra	2	5033	5907
6.	Canara Bank	41	74037	37511
7.	Central Bank of India	54	62533	31441
8.	Corporation Bank	6	13096	6672
9.	Dena Bank	3	4473	22156
10.	Indian Bank	45	44046	15321
11.	Indian Overseas Bank	77	110009	85806
12.	Oriental Bank of Commerce	10	36858	18831
13.	Panjab and Sind Bank	2	2731	1952
14.	State Bank of India	480	974805	635382
15.	State Bank of Bikaner and Jaipur	2	1537	1868
16.	State Bank of Hyderabad	5	8033	3667
17.	State Bank of Travancore	1	2454	2543
18.	State Bank of Mysore	1	4173	3375
19.	Syndicate Bank	29	40414	24967
20.	Union Bank	49	121718	71712
21.	United Bank of India	95	102083	47276
22.	UCO Bank	155	272496	181155
23.	Vijaya Bank	7	14803	6274
	Total Public Sector Banks	**1408**	**2304108**	**1487498**
24.	Centurian Bank	1	5055	2154
25.	Federal Bank	2	7280	3909
26.	HDFC Bank	2	20067	5010
27.	ICICI Bank	6	47631	36816
28.	IDBI Bank	1	4516	232
29.	Karnatak Bank Ltd.	1	2571	4404
30.	Rajasthan Bank Ltd.	1	343	97
31.	Vysya Bank	1	1375	2246
32.	UTI Bank	1	18381	7225
33.	Indus Ind Bank	3	1742	279
	Total Private Sector Banks	**19**	**108961**	**62372**

1	2	3	4	5
34.	Baitarani Gramya Bank	96	37144	24092
35.	Balasore Gramya Bank	62	18480	5430
36.	Bolangir Anch Gramya Bank	149	53590	32057
37.	Cuttack Gramya Bank	121	47757	35894
38.	Dhenkanal Gramya Bank	52	29872	24950
39.	Kalahandi Gramya Bank	76	22563	13353
40.	Koraput Gramya Bank	90	30973	16838
41.	Puri Gramya Bank	113	48563	36795
42.	Rushikulya Gramya Bank	75	35253	19504
	Total of RRBs	**834**	**324195**	**208913**
A	**Total Commercial Banks**	2261	2737264	1758783
43.	Orissa State Co-op. Bank	316	185349	219467
44.	OSCARD Bank	5	-	8087
B	**Total of Co-operative Bank**	321	185349	227554
45.	C.OSFC	-	-	55115
	Grand Total	2582	2922613	2043874

Source: Economy Survey 2005-2006, Government of Orissa, Bhubaneswar.

CONCLUSION

The main drawback of our banks is its failure to sustain its desired credit pattern and to fill the credit gaps in the different sectors of the country. Thus the banking industry is facing a yawning gap between promise and performance and the factor responsible for such a situation is that bank cannot appreciate this new philosophy and new social objective as entrusted by its nationalization. Even after 33 years of nationalization, the nationalized banks still show a great deal of favouritism in advancing loans to big business and established industrialists. In respect of recover of loans, the performance is equally sad. Moreover, bureaucratization, corruption, nepotism, political pressure in granting credit are also affecting the operation of these commercial banks. Trade unions of bank employees and their strike calls have also created a serious threat leading to an economic paralysis. Furthermore, profits of the commercial banks are also showing a declining trend.

REFERENCES

Dhar, P.K., *Indian Economy: Its growing dimensions,* Kalyani Publishers, New Delhi, 2005.

Districts at a Glance, 2006, Government of Orissa, BBSR.*Economic Survey, 2005-06,* Government of Orissa, BBSR.

Ghosh, D.N., *Banking Policy in India,* 2005.

Reserve Bank of India, *Report on Trend and Progress of Banking in India,* 1990-91.

Bank Finance Under Swarnajayanti Gram Swarojgar Yojana (SGSY)

—*Mr. S.K. Badtiya**
—*Dr. R.N. Misra***

INTRODUCTION

Despite efforts made over the part few decades, rural poverty in India continuous to be significant, while the anti-poverty programmes have been strengthened in successive years, and white, in percentage terms, poverty levels have been reduced from 56.44% of India's population in 1973-74 to 37.27% in 1993-94, the number of rural poor has more of less remained static and is estimated to be about 244 million persons. It is in this context that the self-employment programmes assume significance for, they alone can provide income to the rural poor on a sustainable basis. To rectify the situation, Government have decided to restructure the self-employment programmes. A new programme known as "Swarnajayanti Gram Swarozgar Yojana"

* Faculty Member, PGCMS, Dept. of MBA, SMIT, Ankushpur, Berhampur
** Professor Dept of MBA, SMIT, Ankushpur, Berhampur.

(SGSY) has been launched from April-1999. It is a poverty eradication plan by the Government of India to provide self employment through small industries. This is a holistic programme covering all aspects of self-employment such as organization of the poor is to self help groups, training credit, technology, infrastructure and marketing. The plan is a combination of the earlier plans run by the Government of India, such as IRDP, TRYSEM, DWKRA, Ganga Kalyan and the improved Tool Kit Plan. The unspent balance as 01.04.99, under these erstwhile programmes, will be pooled under the head SGSY and utilized as per the new guidelines. SGSY will be funded by the center and the state in the ratio 75.25.

OBJECTIVES

The objective of SGSY will be to bring the assisted poor families (Swarozgaris) above the poverty line in three years, by providing them income generating assets through a mix of Bank Credit and Government subsidy. It would mean ensuring that the family has a monthly net income of at least Rs. 2000/-, subject to availability of funds, the efforts will be to cover 30% of the poor families in each block during the next five years.

FEATURES

Swarnajayanti Gram Swarozgar Yojana aims at established a large number of micro-enterprises in the rural areas, building upon the potential of rural poor. It is rooted in the belief that rural poor in India have competencies and give the right support can be successful products of valuable goods/services.

The assisted families (hence froth known as Swarozgaries) may be individual our groups (Self Help Groups) emphasis will be on the group approach. The objective under SGSY is to bring every assisted family above the poverty line in three years those have monthly income of at least Rs. 2000.

SGSY will particularly focus on the most deprived groups among the rural poor. Accordingly, the SC/STs will account for at lest 50% of the Swarozgaries, women for 40% and the disabled for 30%. Group activity will be given preference and progressively majority of the funds will be for self help groups. At the block level, at least half of the groups will be exclusively women groups.

The Panchayat Samity and the Zilla Parishad or DRDC in association with the banks will identify 4-5 key activities based on the resources, occupational skills of the people and availability of market.

The Bankers play a very critical role in the implementation of SGSY programme right from the identification of key activities, formation and evolution of self-help groups, identifications of individual Swarozgaries as well as planning for all the elements of the key activities. The bank has the final say in the selection of swarozgaries.

For individual loans up to Rs. 50,000 and group loans up to Rs. 3,00,000 lakhs, the assets created out of Bank loan would be hypothecated to the bank as primary security. In cases where moveable assets are not created as in land based activities such as dug well, minor irrigation, etc., mortgage of land may be obtained else third party guarantee may be obtained at the discretion of the bank.

SCOPE AND LIMITATION OF STUDY

The different banks in Orissa played very important role in financing SGSY in Orissa. Due to want of time, the scope of study limited to finance made by the SGSY scheme is taken into consideration. For the purpose of the study only secondary data are taken for the year 2002-03 to 2005-06. So all the limitation of secondary data are found in this study. Due to non availabilities of information, no comparison has been made by other programmes of the Government of Orissa. The scope of the study is limited to bank finance only in the sate of Orissa for Swarnajayanti Gram Swarojgar Yojana.

ANALYSIS OF THE STUDY

Number of beneficiaries, credit subsidy and disburse-ment under SGSY for the year 2000-2001 to 2005-2006, in the State of Orissa is illustrated in the Table 10.1.

Table 10.1: The No. of beneficiaries, Credit Sanction, Subsidy is granted during the year 2000-01 to 2005-2006.

Rs. in Crores

Year	No. of Benefi-ciaries	Credit	Subsidy	Total Disburse ment	Credit and Subsidy Ratio
2000-2001	81721	73.24	45.40	118.64	1.61
2001-2002	59233	52.40	30.23	82.63	1.73
2002-2003	48925	68.89	40.68	109.57	1.69
2003-2004	59289	77.90	49.20	127.10	1.58
2004-2005	65712	97.50	59.41	156.91	1.64
2005-2006	63904	106.98	59.48	166.46	1.79

Source: Economic Survey of Orissa from 2001-2002 to 2006-2007.

Table 10.1 shows us the details of disbursements of funds by banks under SGSY scheme in Orissa for the period 2000-01 to 2005-06. it can be observed from the above table that the total disbursement of funds increases every year from 2001-'02 to 2005-06 Rs. 118.64 to Rs. 166.46 crores respectively. But the no of beneficiaries decreases from 81,721 in 2000-2001 to 48,925 in the year 2002-2003 and again increases 65,721 in the year 2004-2005. In the year 2005-2006 it decreases to 63,904. In the year 2005-06 though the beneficiaries decreases still the disbursement of fund increases from 156.91 crores to 166.46 crore in 2005-2006. Each year finance made to SGSY Scheme is increases except 2001-2002 due to decreases of no of beneficiaries, the total fund also decreases from 118.64 to 82.63 crores.

Different Banks of Orissa Financing under SGSY Scheme during the year 2001-2002 to 2005-06 is explained in the Table 10.2

The details of disbursement of funds, number of beneficiaries etc by banks under SGSY scheme of Orissa for the period 2002-2003 to 2005-2006 are illustrated in Table 10.2. It is observed from the table-II, that the total disbursement of funds and no of beneficiaries has increased from 2002 to 2-006. During the 2002-2003 the no of beneficiaries were 27967 in public sector banks the same has been increased to 36609 i.e. 8642 beneficiaries increased the four year. The RRBs of Orissa has financed to 17934 beneficiaries under SGSY scheme du.ing the year 2000-2003 but the same has been increased to 4898 during the tenure of four year 2001-2003 to 2005-2006. Similarly the cooperative bank are able to

Table 10.2: No. of Beneficiaries credit sanctioned subsidy total disbursement credit and Subsidy ratio is granted during the year 2001-2002 to 2005-06 by different banks.

(Rs in crores)

Bank	No. of Beneficiaries	Credit	Subsidy	Total Disbursement	Credit and Subsidy Raito
Public Sector Banks					
2002-2003	27967	40.14	23.12	63.26	1.73
2003-2004	33561	45.49	28.29	73.78	1.60
2004-2005	38371	57.20	34.68	91.88	1.64
2005-2006	36609	61.60	33.96	95.56	1.81
Total	**136508**	**204.43**	**120.05**	**324.48**	**6.78**
Regional Rural Banks					
2002-2003	17934	24.09	14.91	39.00	1.61
2003-2004	21974	27.52	17.66	45.18	1.55
2004-2005	23155	33.27	20.89	54.16	1.59
2005-2006	22832	37.02	21.51	58.53	1.71
Total	**85,895**	**121.90**	**74.97**	**196.87**	**6.46**

Co-operative Banks					
2002-2003	3024	4.67	2.65	7.32	1.76
2003-2004	3754	4.89	3.26	8.14	1.5
2004-2005	4186	7.03	3.84	10.87	1.83
2005-2006	4463	8.36	4.01	12.37	2.08
Total	**15427**	**24.95**	**13.76**	**38.70**	**7.17**

Source: From *Economics survey of Orissa from 2002-2003 to 2005-2006.*

finance to 3024 beneficiaries under the SGSY scheme during the year 2002-2003 but the same has been increased to 4463 beneficiaries in the year 2005-2006. So during this four year 1439 beneficiaries has been increased with comparison to year 2002-2003 to 2005-2006. So from the table it is found that all the beneficiaries are increased with reference to the Public Sector Bank, Regional Rural Bank and Co-operative Banks.

During the 2002-2003 the total disbursement of funds were 63.26 crores by public sector banks the same has been increased to 95.56 crores i.e. 32.30 crores has been increased during the four years. The Regional Rural Banks of Orissa also has financed of Rs. 39.00 crore under SGSY Scheme during the year 2002-2003 but the same has been increased to 58.53 crores in the year 2005-2006 i.e. 19.53 crores has been financed during the tenure years from 2002-2003 to 2005-2006. Similarly the co-operative Bank are also finance of Rs. 7.32 crores under the SGSY Scheme during the year 2002-2003 but the same has been increased to 12.37 crores in the 2005-2006. So during this year 5.05 crores has been increased with comparison to the year 2002-2003 to 2005-2006. So from the Table 10.2 it is found that all the banks have increased their finance towards SGSY schemes.

It has been seen from Table 10.2 that the credit subsidy ratio of public Sector Banks has increased from 1.73 to 1.81 during the year 2002-2003 to 2005-2006. But the same has been showed in decreasing trend in 2003-2004. During 2003-2004 and 2004-2005 the credit subsidy ratio (1.60) decreased (1.55 during the year 2003-2004 and 1.59 during the year

2004-2005). In case of Regional Rural banks credit subsidy ratio also increased from 1.61 to 1.71 during the all four year but it has been reduced to 1.55 in the year 2003-2004 in comparison to the year 2002-2003. In case of Co-operatives Banks this ratio has been decreases to 1.50 in the year 2003-2004 from 1.76 in comparison to same has been showed in decreasing trend in 2003-2004. During 2003-2004 and 2004-2005 the credit subsidy ratio (1.60) decreases (1.55 during the year 2003-2004 1.59 during the year 2004-2005). In case of Regional Rural Banks credit subsidy ratio also increased from 1.61 to 1.71 during the all four year but it has been reduced to 1.55 in the year 2003-2004 in comparison to the year 2002-2003. In case of Co-operative Banks this ratio has been decreases to 1.50 in the year 2003-2004 from 1.76 in comparison to the year 2002-2003. It again increased to 1.81 and 2.08 in the year 2004-2005 and 2005-2006 respectively.

CONCLUSION

Investment occupies a central position in the development of the economy, the investment made through institution sources contribute to the process of capital accumulation. Considering the role of these institution in the economy development of country, no doubt it is found to be significant. The Swarnajayanti Swarojgar Yojana (SGSY) was established in the year 1999 with responsibility assigned by the Government for providing adequate, timely and easy credit to the small and medium entrepreneur in the state for economic development of the people.

During the year 2000-2001 the Government of Orissa has able to fiancé 81,721 beneficiaries but the same has decreased to 59,233 during the year 2001-2002 and again during the year 2005-2006 it has decreased to 63,904. Similarly in total disbursement often 2000-2001 the total disbursement of fund was 118.6 crores but it has been decreased to 82.63 crores during the year 2001-2002 but in all the year it shows in increasing trend. The credit subsidy ratio watch 1.61 during the year 2000-2001 but all the years it shows an increasing trend and it was 1.79 during the year 2005-2006. all the Banks i.e. PSBs, RRBs, Cooperative Banks financed Rupees 324.48 crores, Rs. 196.87 crores, Rs. 38.70 crores respectively during all the four years of the study. But the beneficiaries as well as total disbursement has decreased during the year 2005-2006 in comparison to year 2004-2005 except Cooperative Banks.

Index

A

Agricultural credit 16, 91

Andhra Pradesh 43, 54

Annual Budget 91

B

Badtiya, S.K. 141

Bank Finance under SGSY 141
- analysis of the study 144
- features 142
- introduction 141
- objectives 142
- scope and limitation 144

Bank loan amount 10

Basmati rice 108

Bihar 49

C

Central Government 28

Changing Pattern of Panchayat Finance in Orissa 120
- Eleventh Finance Commission Grants
  - District Level 125
  - Gram Panchayat Level 128
  - State Finance Commission Grants and PRIs 124
- Methodology 125
- organizational structure of pris 121
- plan proposal to strengthen pris 123
- policy suggestions 130
- SFC recommendation and panchayat finances 129

Chicago Mercantile Exchange 107, 108

Commercial banks 17, 28, 46

Commodities futures trading 108

Commodity derivative 103

Co-operative banks 15, 32, 80

Co-operative credit societies 16, 17, 20

Credit 39

Crop insurance 90

D

Dash, Satyabrat 38

Deo, Malabika 57

Dependence of rural households 44

Derivatives 102-110

District rural development agencies 122

Districts Central Co-operative Banks 19

Dr. L.C. Gupta Committee 109

DWKRA 142

E

Eleventh Finance Commission 124
  grants to blocks in Ganjam District 126
Exchange derivatives 106

F

Farmers 15
Fertilizers 15
Financial derivative 103
Financial derivative after globalisation 101
  cash settlement 114
  classification of financial derivative 103
  clearing corporation 113
  convertibles 116
  daily settlement and margin/stock broker 113
  delivery 114
  financial derivatives in India 110
  forward contract 110
  future contract 112
  history of derivatives markets 107
  introduction 101
  objective and scope of the study 102
  options contracts 114
  standardization 112
  SWAP 117
  tick size 113
  types of derivatives 103
    components of derivative 104
    feature of a financial derivative 105
    purpose of the derivatives 104
  use of derivatives 117
  warrants 116
Financial institutions 28
Financial institutions in economic development of Orissa 27
  commercial banks 28
  co-operative banks 32
  non-banking organisations 34
  regional rural banks 31
Financial services in Orissa 134
Financing the self-help groups by the financial institutions 1
  analysis of the study 5
  brief profile of the sample district 4
  limitations of the study 4
  methodology 5
  objective of the study 3
French 60

G

Gadgil Committee 14
Gajapati District of Odisha 4
Ganga Kalyan 142
Ganjam district 4
GDP 39
Gibbons 60
Globalisation 39
Government 17
Government of India 14, 55, 91
Gram Panchayat 121
Ground level credit 81
Growth of SHGs in India 5, 7
Gujarat 54

I

Indian banking system 135
Institutional credit 20
Institutional credit and agricultural development in Orissa 79
  adequacy of farm credit 86
  crop insurance 90
  demand syndromes of institutional credit in orissa 92
  doubling of credit 91
  effective demand 93
  ground level credit flow 81
  institutional credit scenario 79
  kissan credit cards 88
  micro-finance 90
  natural calamities 95
  overdue and NPAs 96
  rural infrastructure development fund 91
  supply syndrome of institutional credit 86
Institutional credit scenario 79
Institutional credits 86, 92
Institutional sources of agricultural credit 16
Insurance services 47
International monetary market 107
IRDP 2, 55
Istanbul Stock Exchange 61

K

Kissan credit Cards 88, 92
Kumar, Harish 57

L

Land development banks 17
Landlords 18
Liberalization 39
Loan granted by different banks to the SHG 9
Loans granted to the SHGs 8
Local self-government 120
London International Financial Futures Exchange 108
Looms 40

M

Mahalwary 14
Maharashtra 54
Management of Financial Services in Orissa 134
  India 135
  Orissa 134
Marginal and small farmers 93
Medium and large landholdings 93
Micro-finance in India 38
  alternative micro finance institutions 48
  borrower unfriendly products and procedures 50
  demand for savings and insurance services 42
  – of micro finance services in india 39
  demands for credit 40
  financing to alternative mfis 51
  high transaction costs, both legitimate and illegal 51
  inflexibility and delay 51
  legal and regulatory framework 51
  mainstream micro-finance institutions 48

supply of micro-finance services 43
micro-finance institutional structure 48
moving forward 55
problems associated with mainstream mfis 50
– for alternative micro-finance institutions 52
inappropriate legal forms 53
lack of commercial orientation 54
lack of proper governance and accountability 55
isolated and scattered 55
share of debt from institutional and non-institutional sources 45
social obligation and not a business opportunity 51
supply of savings and insurance services 47
Micro-enterprises 10
Micro-Finance Institutions 48, 53, 54
Mishra, Rabi Narayana 1, 13, 38, 141
Money-lenders 16, 18

N

NABARD 2, 3, 51, 52, 86, 90
Nayak, Bibhudatta 79
Nayak, Sudhansu Sekhar 13
Nifty 67
Non-banking finance companies 49
Non-banking organizations 34
Non-farm activities 41
NYSE 64

O

Orissa Gram Panchayat Act, 1948 121
Orissa State Co-operative Agricultural Rural Development Bank 19
Orissa State Co-operative Bank 19

P

Panchayat 121
Panchayat Samities 122, 143
Pattnaik, Biju 122
Patra, Anita 1
Patro, Bhagabata 120
Patro, Biswanath 101
Pattnaik, Kishore Chandra 120
PR institutions 120
Pradhan, Sudhir 101

R

Rajasthan 49
Rashtriya Gramin Vikas Nidhi 50
RBI 54, 109
Regional Rural Banks 17, 31, 46
Regularities in Indian stock market 57
analysis and discussion 67
data and period of the study 64
hypothesis 67
implication for market efficiency 73
methodology 65
pattern of deviation 71
previous studies 60

testing for statistical significance
equality of returns 67
Relatives 18
Reliance 115
Renewal Credit Survey Committee 14
Reserve Bank of India 43, 135
Role of Cooperative Banks in Financing Agricultural Credit in Orissa 13
scope and objective of the study 14
about agricultural credit 15
types of agricultural credit 15
long-term credit 16
medium-term credit 16
short-term credit 15
sources of agricultural credit 16
institutional sources 16
non-institutional sources 18
analysis 19
year-wise position of agricultural credit cooperative societies 20
sector-wise distribution of institutional credit 20
targets and achievement of institutional credit 23
suggestions 23
Rural Infrastructure Development Fund 91
Ryotwari 14

S

Sahu, Anil Kumar 134
Sahu, Bibhu Prasad 120
Sarma, R.P. 27
Sarva Jana Seva Kosh Ltd 49
Satyam 115
SBI 115
Securities 109
Self-employment programmes 141
Self-help groups 3
SENSEX 64, 67
SIDBI 52
Sodhani Expert Group 109
Sources of Credit for Rural Households 44
State Finance Commis-sion 124
Stock market 62
Swarnajayanti Gram Swarozgar Yojana 141-144
Swarozgaris 142, 143

T

Tamil Nadu 49
Tata Steel 115
Term Loan 86
Tool Kit Plan 142
Traders and Commission Agents 18
TRYSEM 142

U

U.K. 14
U.S.A 14
Urban Co-operative Banks 19

W

Woman marginal workers 42

Z

Zamindari system 14
Zilla Parishad 122, 143

❑❑❑